W9-CHA-713

ADVENTURES IN PERSIA

Ordeal of the Hassanabad Pass

Adventures in Persia

TO INDIA BY THE BACK DOOR

RONALD SINCLAIR

H. F. & G. WITHERBY LTD

First published in Great Britain 1988 by
H. F. & G. WITHERBY LTD,
14 Henrietta Street, London WC2E 8QJ

British Library Cataloguing in Publication Data
Sinclair, Ronald, *1889–*
Adventures in Persia.
1. Iran. Journeys by cars, 1925–1941
I. Title
915.5′052

ISBN 0-85493-173-2

Typeset by Centracet
and printed in Great Britain by
St Edmundsbury Press Ltd,
Bury St Edmunds, Suffolk

CONTENTS

INTRODUCTORY NOTE

by Sir John Gardener, KCMG

In his book *Adventures in Persia* Ronald Sinclair, an experienced traveller in the Middle East, gives us a most interesting and happy account of his journey by motor-car, alone (instead of in the usual convoy), from the Mediterranean to India, at a time when the car was still a rarity in that region, and motor roads, garages, etc. had still to be developed.

Wisely avoiding technicalities, the author concentrates on the human aspects of his journey. Possessing a light, but able pen and a thorough knowledge of the languages concerned, Ronald Sinclair draws a fascinating and (if I may say so) accurate pen picture of people and of a region which, though in the recent past, still possesses charm and interest for all of us, whether students of the Middle East or not.

Nor does his book lack the interest of adventures, both comic and serious, which on two occasions nearly ended in disaster.

Exmouth

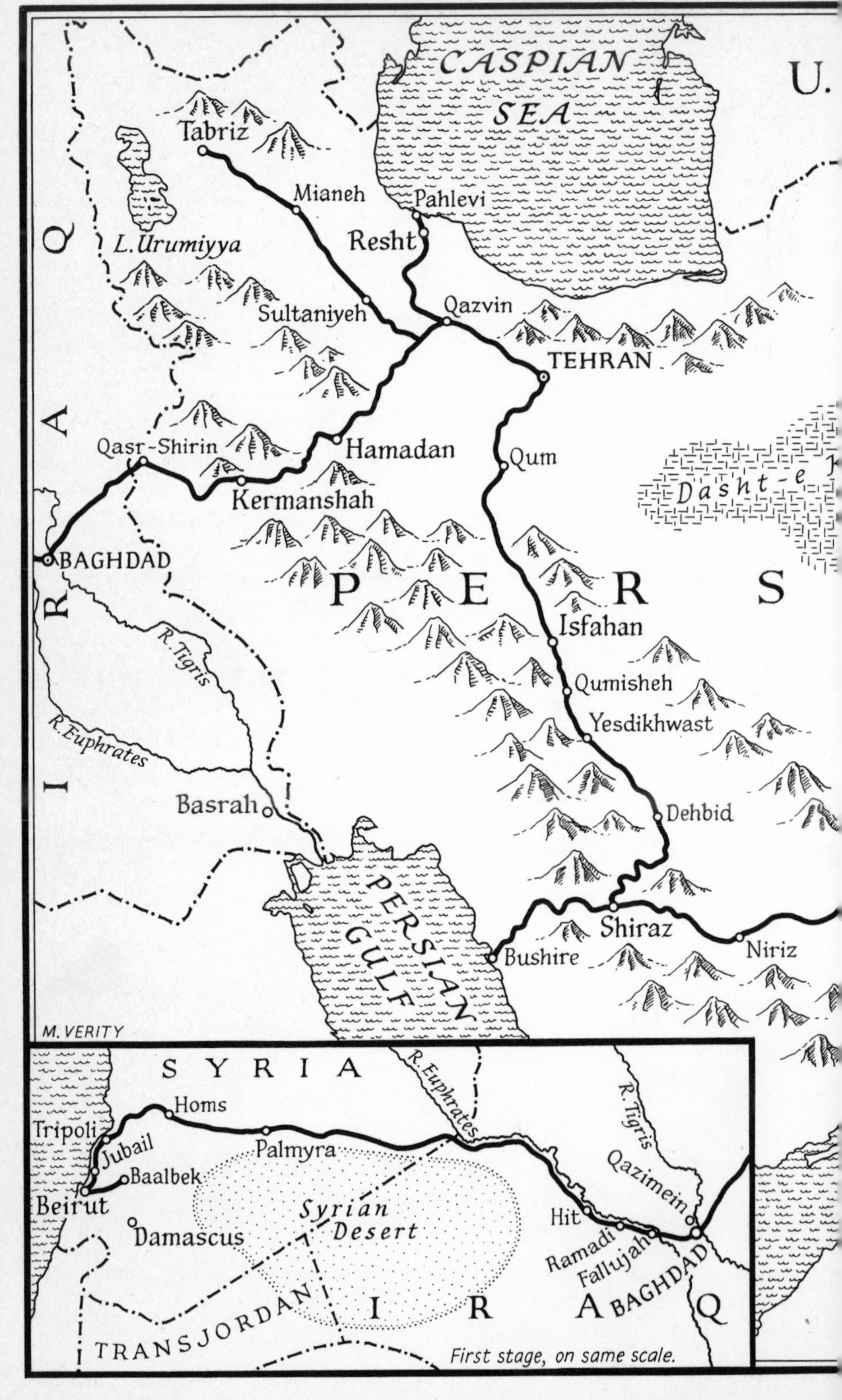
CASPIAN
SEA
U.
Tabriz
Mianeh
Pahlevi
Resht
L. Urumiyya
Sultaniyeh
Qazvin
TEHRAN
Hamadan
Qasr-Shirin
Kermanshah
Qum
Dasht-e
BAGHDAD
P E R S
Isfahan
R. Tigris
Qumisheh
Yesdikhwast
R. Euphrates
Basrah
Dehbid
PERSIAN GULF
Shiraz
Bushire
Niriz
I R A Q
M. VERITY
SYRIA
Homs
Tripoli
Jubail
Palmyra
Baalbek
Beirut
Damascus
Syrian Desert
R. Euphrates
R. Tigris
Qazimein
Hit
Ramadi
Fallujah
BAGHDAD
I R A Q
TRANSJORDAN
First stage, on same scale.

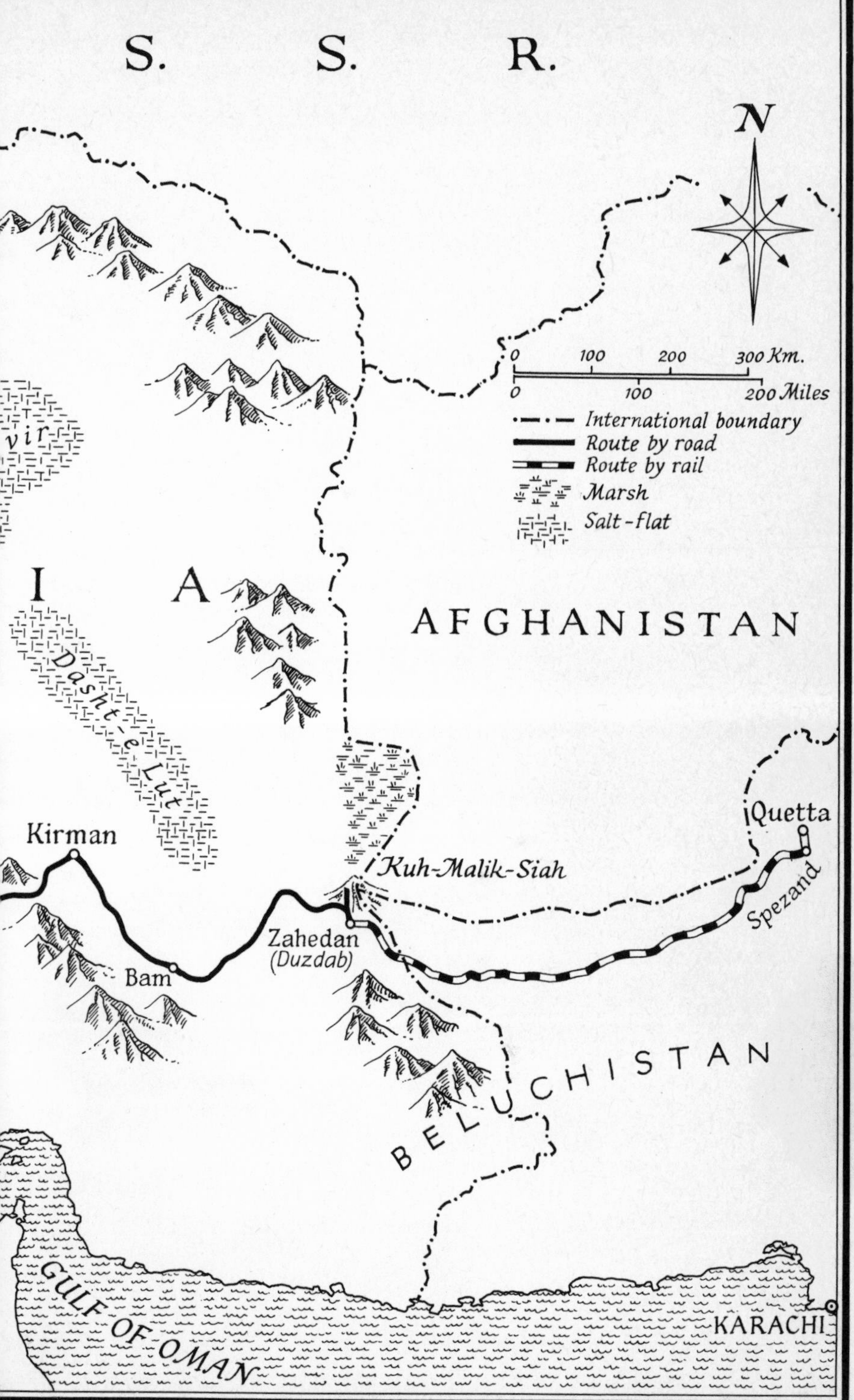

S. S. R.
N
0 100 200 300 Km.
0 100 200 Miles
International boundary
Route by road
Route by rail
Marsh
Salt-flat
vir
I A
AFGHANISTAN
Dasht-e-Lut
Kirman
Quetta
Kuh-Malik-Siah
Spezand
Zahedan
(Duzdab)
Bam
BELUCHISTAN
GULF OF OMAN
KARACHI

PRELUDE

I switched off the motor for the hundredth and possibly the last time. The sun was right overhead, the cloudless sky leaden and heavy with heat. The sand was burning to the touch. The only shade was underneath the car. In every direction the desert was flat and endless, the landscape unbroken, with nothing to be seen but the quivering waves of over-heated air and mirage. Not a whisper of a breeze, only the heat-waves danced unceasingly, everything else was motionless and dead. The only animal life I had seen all day had been a few small desert lizards. I had not sighted a single bird, not even a vulture, but if I came to grief they would be round in flocks and would make short work of me.

Anyway, there was nothing more I could do. The wheels of the car were hopelessly embedded in the powder-like sand and the more I tried to clear them, the deeper they sank in. Once again I scanned my surroundings, but I could see no horizon, nor discern where desert ended and sky began. I had a splitting headache. God, how it ached. Could it be heat-stroke? Keep calm, I kept telling myself. I was by now completely exhausted. I lay down beside the car and drew the heavy tarpaulin over my head and body to get what shade I could. I shut my eyes tightly to ease the throbbing in my head, and I tried to reason things out calmly. It was difficult to concentrate. I knew that I had only myself to blame for my present helpless predicament, but I began now to regret that Jim Bradley had ever got me into this assignment.

It had all sounded so attractive when he told me of the important group of manufacturers in England who wanted to send a man out to Iran to study and report on trading conditions there. They had asked the Board of Trade if they could recommend any person with the right qualifications and the enquiry had been passed to Jim Bradley's department.

Jim must have recommended me strongly for I was given a friendly reception at my meeting with the directors. They explained that they wanted a person with experience in Persia, someone who could speak the language, to go out and visit the principal towns and business centres and send home reports on market conditions and trade possibilities in general. I could decide what places to visit and how I travelled. For expenses I could draw on credits in the Imperial Bank of Persia, and the bank had been asked to instruct their local managers to accord me any assistance I needed.

The terms offered were generous and altogether it was a most tempting assignment. I accepted without hesitation. It was agreed that I should have two weeks in which to make my preparations. My new colleagues stood me an excellent farewell luncheon, I shook hands all round, they wished me luck.

It was the middle of January when I took the train from London to Genoa, and from there an Italian steamer landed me at Beirut.

Chapter 1

BEIRUT

I had just one good friend in Beirut, Emil Mattar, and before boarding the steamer in Genoa I had dashed off a short cable announcing my impending arrival and had asked him to reserve me accommodation for a short visit.

As the ship edged in to its berthing place in Beirut, I was delighted to see Emil waiting at the dockside. We greeted each other warmly.

'I've booked you a room at Bassoul's,' he said. 'It's not one of the big modern hotels, for I didn't think you wanted anything like that. It's a bit old-fashioned, no swimming-pool, but it's comfortable, the food and service are good, the terms moderate. Also the proprietor is a friend of mine and will take good care of you.' I thanked him and said it would suit me just fine. He said it was close to the business quarter, just a short stroll from the docks.

Landing formalities were simple and quickly completed. Within a few minutes we were on our way, with a couple of porters carrying my baggage. Away from the immediate vicinity of the harbour we paused to admire the magnificent view that now unfolded itself before us.

Rising from sea-level, the old town spreads upwards and appears to melt into the luxuriant expanse covering the lower mountain slopes in a mantle of countless different colours. One could pick out patches of dark-green orange trees, mingling with the lighter green lemon foliage and still lighter green of larches, contrasting with walnut, oak, sycamore, and the silvery-tipped crests of olive trees. There were acres and acres of hillside decked in flowering shrubs, with splashes of vivid colour from scattered gardens belonging to bluish-white villas, whose bright-red roofs added to the almost breath-taking beauty of the landscape. As we approached the fringes of the town, I felt very much reminded of Constantinople and in particular of old Stamboul. A policeman at a street corner was still wearing the old Turkish police uniform, complete with the familiar *kalpak*, and in his hand was a baton resembling a miniature barber's pole with red and white stripes. From his rather sloppy appearance he might have stepped straight from a similar street corner in Stamboul.

I mentioned this to Emil, who laughed and said, 'Well, don't forget that the Turks were here for long periods and left their mark in many more ways than just policemen. These *hamals*, for instance, are all Kurds.'

'Why, so they are,' I said, 'I hadn't really noticed them until they started piling up all that baggage. They used to amaze me in Constantinople with the tremendous weights they could carry. There's a street in Constantinople we used to call Step Street, very steep and narrow and leads up from near the Bosphorus past the Galata tower into Pera. It was composed almost entirely of steps. Walking down one day I watched four Kurd *hamals* coming up, and what d'you think they were carrying? A grand piano, full size, and complete, except for its legs which they had screwed off. And how were they carrying it? Why, on their heads, of course. I stepped aside to let them pass, and saw that they had nothing but a small coil of canvas stuffed with cotton to ease the pressure on their skulls. They passed at a steady funereal pace, wisely wasting no oxygen in needless conversation, and pausing only at rare intervals for a few brief moments to ease their lungs.'

Within a further five minutes' walking we reached the hotel, with the heavily laden *hamals* at our heels. They quickly divested themselves of their loads and placed them in a big pile at the side of the main entrance. Emil paid them off, as I had not yet got any local currency. There was no haggling over payment. None of that whining and wheedling 'You pay me dollars, Sahib' that one gets in India and elsewhere on the world's tourist routes. Emil's Arabic showed that we were not tourists. The Kurds accepted what they were given with a dignified nod, and departed.

Now, as I looked at the equivalent of a full mule-load of baggage, a sturdily built, square-shouldered individual in a dark suit appeared in the doorway like a *deus ex machina*, and greeted us with a broad friendly smile, revealing a wealth of gold teeth. Emil introduced him as Mr Henry Bassoul, the proprietor of the hotel. We shook hands and I nearly winced at the pressure of his powerful grasp. 'Welcome to Beirut,' he said, 'and to my hotel. As a friend of Mr Mattar you are specially welcome.' In appearance he might have been a southern Italian, a Greek, a Maltese or what one might call a non-semitic Mediterranean. I judged him to be in his late fifties.

'You speak very good English,' I told him. He replied. 'I learned it as a barman in South Kensington. You'll like my bar, you'll imagine you're back in England. I suggest you go and make yourselves comfortable in there. Dinner will be served any time between 7.30 and 10.00 P.M. and the bar closes at midnight, unless specially requested, and of course it is open all day. Not like in England. You'll find a good variety of every kind of drink in there, wine, spirits and good English beer, but most of my English clients prefer lager, which seems to suit our warmer climate better than your heavier British ale. Jim the barman will be happy to look after you.'

In the bar one could see that a brave attempt had been made to create a British atmosphere, though the effect was perhaps half-way between that of a club and a pub. A number of dark leather-covered armchairs, well worn but still presentable, lured the customer to sit or slumber. Framed, brightly coloured scenes of fox-hunting and other sporting subjects adorned the walls and an oaken side-table displayed a variety of illustrated journals and newspapers in English, French and several other languages. Both the floor and the counter were of polished cedar or possibly stained pine-wood, and a number of tall-legged stools were lined up invitingly along the counter.

Jim, the barman, a New Zealander ex-serviceman who, like some others of his countrymen, had decided to remain in Lebanon after the war, greeted us cheerfully and as we sank into a couple of armchairs, we unanimously ordered two chilled lagers.

Emil produced his cigarette case and offered me one. 'They're Turkish. You may not care for them?'

'I'm not a heavy smoker,' I said, 'but I've always had a preference for Turkish cigarettes.' I took one and he lit for both of us. I raised my glass. He raised his. 'Cheers, and welcome to Beirut. I've always hoped to see you here one day.' 'Cheers,' I replied, 'and I'm delighted to be here. You know, Emil, now that I come to look at you closely, you don't seem to have changed a bit, or very little, since we last met in London three years ago.' I knew from what he had then told me that he must now be in his mid-thirties, but now he did not look a bit older than twenty-eight.

He had handsome, regular features and clear grey eyes. His hair was dark brown, as were also his thick-arched eyebrows. He was a full six feet tall, broad-shouldered, with narrow hips and the figure of an athlete. He must have caused many a flutter among the other sex. I was surprised he had not already got married, but I did not care to mention it.

'And now that you *are* here, how long do you plan to stay? I hope that you'll stay at least a reasonable time.'

'That depends upon what you call a reasonable time. It'll be at least a few days until I can arrange some transport to Baghdad. You see, my destination is really Persia, but I have to get to Baghdad first and go on from there.'

Emil's face fell. 'But surely you don't have to rush away. Persia is an ancient country and it isn't going to disappear overnight. Beirut is only a port, but the surrounding country is chock full of history and I was planning to do a whole series of trips and show you a number of places you really ought to see.' His disappointment was so genuine that I relented and said that I promised to spend all the time with him that I possibly could. 'The fact is simply,' I told him, 'that I have a certain job to do, but it relates entirely to Persia and not to the Lebanon. It's quite a big job and it's going to take some time. If you care to listen, I'll tell you what it's all about. And then I think you'll understand why I must lose no time in getting on with it.' We settled back in our chairs and I told him briefly the story of my assignment. Emil listened in silence, now and then each of us taking sips of our lager.

'And that's the whole story,' I said finally. 'I don't know how it will end, but I suppose I'll make my way back to England, probably by the same way I came.'

'Anyway it's some consolation that we will have the possibility of getting together when you do come back, and I can only hope you will be able to stay longer next time.'

'I'll certainly try to do so,' I said. 'By the way, how many languages do you speak, Emil?'

He laughed. 'Not as many as I know you speak.'

'I mean, how many do you actually use?'

'Well, French, naturally, because it is really the official language. Arabic, of course, because it is the country's mother tongue. More and more Arabs are picking up English, or mainly Yankee slang from the "movies", but one can carry on with English, French and Arabic. I find it useful to speak Greek, as I meet so many Greeks in everyday business. I also have a smattering of Italian. I can remember, before the war, Italian was the most commonly spoken foreign language, but the French have tried so hard to make French compulsory that Italian has been pushed into the background.'

'Generally speaking, would you say the French are popular?'

Emil smiled. 'If you were not just rushing through Beirut, you would soon learn the answer to that one, but we don't talk about it, except among friends. In Syria the French are particularly disliked. Here they are tolerated. Here we just accept things as they are, and mind our own business. I try to avoid politics. It isn't always easy, but it is much safer.'

I felt I was treading on delicate ground, and discreetly changed the subject.

'Emil, do please tell me something about this Mr Nairn,

whom I am hoping to meet. I have, of course, heard a certain amount, but I've never learned the whole story of what he actually did that made him so famous.'

'Well, it's rather a long story, but I'll try to tell you briefly. Norman Nairn is a New Zealander and was here in the Air Force during the war. On completing his military service he remained here and concentrated his attention upon proving or disproving his belief that it should be possible to traverse the desert between Beirut and Baghdad by wheeled transport. He was supported by a wealthy Arab merchant named Ibn Bassam, who had amassed a considerable fortune smuggling gold between Damascus and Baghdad by camel, following secret routes known only to himself.

'Nairn developed his acquaintance with Ibn Bassam, and the latter accompanied him on a exploratory trip eastward across the desert. They made surprising progress and satisfied themselves that there were no insuperable obstacles to wheeled traffic on the 630 miles of desert to Baghdad.

'Then, encouraged by this discovery, and backed by the Iraqi government, Nairn made a further crossing in May 1923, as a result of which he gained a five-year contract for the carriage of mails between Baghdad and Haifa, where they were loaded onto a train for Port Said, reaching there within 60 hours as compared with 24 days by the sea route.

'The French were so impressed by this success that they granted Nairn their contract for mails between Damascus and Baghdad. In addition, Nairn now inaugurated a passenger service between Baghdad and the Mediterranean which was more comfortable and much cheaper than going by air.

'The Nairn organisation was extremely efficient. At first their weekly convoy comprised only two cars; now they have a dozen. In 1924 Nairn hired no less than eleven extra cars to carry the Shah and his suite across the desert. This added greatly to Nairn's reputation for reliability and security, and result in so much competition that the Iraqi and the Syrian governments forbade single cars to attempt the crossing for fear of breakdown and attack by Bedouins. Many Arabs ignored this ban and slipped away stealthily, but lost themselves and were never heard of again. Despite patrols by Iraqi Levies, Rolls-Royce armoured cars and Bristol fighters, Bedouin attacks have continued and still remain a constant danger. Every Nairn car carries two drivers, always British ex-servicemen. They have the reputation of never letting their passengers down and their endurance and devotion have become famous throughout the Middle East.

'With the Iraqi mail contract Nairn's were financially sound, but they were not subsidised by the British Government in spite of the acknowledged value of their services. This was because they steadfastly refused to purchase and use British vehicles, for the good reason that none existed that were able to withstand the terrific strain of the desert route. Not only were the British cars too expensive, they were too low-built to clear the many obstacles, they had not the power to carry the tremendous loads habitually piled upon the Nairn machines at anything like the very high speeds demanded of them, were too heavy to be easily hauled out of mud, and inadequately cooled. American cars were not so handicapped.

'A serious set-back to Nairn was the loss early last year [1925] of the Syrian mail contract. The organisation that won this contract away from Nairn was the Eastern Transport Company, run by Syrians and subsidised by the French Government in order to compete with Nairn. The ETC usually ran their cars over the Palmyra-Kubaisa route, where there were hotels, but on occasion used the more direct Rutba route. In addition they held a monopoly of the motor route beyond Baghdad and ran a fortnightly passenger service to the Persian capital Tehran. Despite these advantages Nairn's was vastly superior in general efficiency and the latest development is that Nairn's and the ETC have amalgamated under the name Nairn Eastern Transport Company, with Nairn holding a major interest and the French Government a junior partner. The company's activities have now increased to a point where the British Government has acquired a substantial measure of indirect control through the holdings of various major banks.'

At this moment, Jim the barman sidled up to Emil and

half-whispered, 'Excuse me, sir, but I think you wanted to meet Mr Nairn. Well, he's just coming in now.'

We rose to our feet as a well-built, sun-burned individual in khaki drill bush jacket and shorts entered the bar. He waved a greeting hand at Emil who signed to him to come over and join us, while Jim pushed up a third armchair and an extra small table, and Emil ordered 'Three chilled lagers, please Jim,' and almost in the same breath added 'I want you to meet an old friend of mine, Ron Sinclair. Ron wants to consult you, he has a problem, and I told him you're the best man to advise him.'

'Glad to help you if I can,' Nairn turned to me and grasped my hand firmly as I looked into a pair of clear blue eyes, their colour enhanced by the dark sun-burn. 'Let's sit down and have a sip first. I've just come from a conference with the French police and political people, and with their English and my equally poor French, it was pretty hot work and my throat's as dry as a bone.'

Emil produced his cigarettes. Nairn took one and he and Emil lit up. I declined and we all sipped our lager.

'The French are worried,' Nairn went on. 'They've got fresh trouble on their hands with the Druze, who've been sniping at motor traffic again. Just a few young hot-heads involved, probably, but the French have had enough, and are out to teach the Druze a lesson, or so they say. Anyway, we're having to direct the next convoy by the northern route via Homs and Palmyra.'

'This will affect you, Ron,' Emil said, 'but it may give you a little time in Beirut.' He turned to Nairn. 'He's anxious to get to Baghdad and then on to Persia. I begged him not hurry, and assured him that Persia would not disappear overnight and that he'd do better to spend a little time and buy a car here instead of in Baghdad.'

'Well, you know your friend may be right about Persia disappearing.' Nairn smiled and his eyes twinkled mischievously. 'I hear that Reza Shah is seriously planning to give the country back its ancient name of Iran, banning the use of the word Persia and Persian and expunging it from all maps and public notices, but I suppose we can go on using the old name until the decree actually comes out.

'And what's your problem, Mr Sinclair?' He turned to me, and I told of my assignment and my idea of buying a car in Baghdad.

'Buy a car? Yes, I think you should, but not in Baghdad. There you would find very little choice and the prices are exorbitant. You should definitely make your purchase here in Beirut. There are several reliable dealers, you should have a good look round. Take your time over it until you find exactly what you need.'

'I gave him the name of Shukri's garage,' Emil said, 'I've always found him very reasonable and reliable.'

'Yes, I would also recommend Shukri. Mention that we have sent you to him and I'm sure he'll give you a square deal. You might also mention that you'll be driving across the desert and that you hear that the police are tightening up their inspections. I'm sure he knows all about it and won't sell you anything the police won't approve. If you can't find what you want at Shukri's, let me know and I'll get my people to make enquiries elsewhere.'

Norman Nairn glanced at his wrist-watch, then with an exclamation quickly got to his feet, picked up his glass and drained it. 'Thanks for the drink, I must be off,' he said. 'I'm sorry to have to leave you fellows, we must meet again and continue our talk. Fact is, I have to be on the line to New York in exactly half an hour. I can just make it. Goodbye for the present, and Mr Sinclair, do not hesitate to call on our manager if you need anything. I'll tell him to do everything he can for you. Goodbye now, and best of luck on your trip.' Next moment he was gone.

Early next morning I found Shukri's garage. An Arab mechanic pointed out the *patron*, a comfortable-looking Lebanese in his mid-forties, with the incipient abdominal bulge which in this part of the world is usually a sign of prosperity.

He greeted me in French and his face expanded into a

friendly smile when I told him Nairn and Mattar had sent me. I explained what I wanted to do and asked his advice. He thought for a few moments, then said he might have just what I required and led me across the big courtyard which had once been a caravanserai.

'There,' he pointed to a small shiny black car parked away in a corner. It was an A-model Ford, first cousin to the famous model-T. I was intrigued by the name ZOBEIDA painted in neat white letters on one door. He explained that the car had belonged to a French officer who had been transferred. It had not run many kilometres and was almost new. The price was low, he said, because the Lebanese preferred big powerful cars which could run up the mountain roads in top gear. He assured me that for Iran the small Ford was more suitable. He himself had been up there and knew that country. Except in the few large cities, there were no facilities for repairs or servicing, and the extra high clearance of this particular model and its light weight were big advantages in rough country.

I thought that a heavier car would hold the road better. Shukri agreed, but pointed out with forcible logic that where there was no road, there was nothing to hold, and that if one got off the track or fell into a ditch, a light car could be pulled out, but with a heavy one, one really would be in a hole.

This seemed to make sense. I took the Ford for a trial run. It behaved quite well and the price was reasonable. So, for better or for worse, Zobeida became mine.

Later that day I drove round to Emil's office. He stared at Zobeida in silence. 'D'you seriously mean that you're going to cross the desert in that?'

'That's the idea,' I said. 'Any objections?'

'Only that I think you're crackers, and I can't understand how Shukri came to sell you such a thing.'

'He did so,' I said, 'because I agreed with him that it was the best car for driving about in a country with no roads.'

'Well, Shukri ought to know,' he said resignedly, 'but it certainly looks a crazy thing to try to cross the desert with.

I'd like to hear what Nairn's manager has to say when he sees it.'

'Don't worry, he's already seen it. I took it round there before coming here. He did think it was a bit on the light side, but it is in excellent condition, and he's almost sure the police will pass it. If they do, he will tell one of his men to keep an eye on me during the trip.'

I had been just about to leave the manager's office when Norman Nairn came in. He was interested to see Zobeida, and agreed she was rather on the light side, but that this could also be an advantage.

He had also given me the latest news about the convoy. It seemed that the French had now told him that they found it necessary to draft in extra men to deal with the additional duties connected with the inspection, especially since there had been a big increase in the cross-desert traffic to Baghdad. For this reason the French would be unable to produce the full quota of police for duty on the regular convoy departure on Wednesday, but could promise to have them in full strength for the convoy to start first thing on Thursday morning. Nairn said he had no doubt but that the French would keep this promise, and that it was quite definite the convoy would take the northern route via Homs and Palmyra rather than the regular one via Damascus.

I thanked Nairn again and said I would look forward to meeting him on my return in a few months' time. He wished me the best of luck and I came away.

Emil expressed great pleasure that I now had at least one extra day for sightseeing, and said that he would be calling for me on the morrow for a trip to Baalbek, and would be bringing his sister and a cousin with him. I told him I would drive the party in my car in order to give Zobeida all the exercise I could in readiness for the desert trip on Thursday.

Chapter 2

BEIRUT TO PALMYRA

It was still dark in the streets, but the sky was turning pearly grey over the mountain crests as I left the hotel and drove off to the assembly point of the cross-desert convoy. The start would be at 6.30 A.M. from the military transport depot, and I was warned to be there soon after daybreak for the police inspection of vehicles. Since this meant rising well before dawn, I had loaded all my belongings onto the car before turning in for the night, after returning from sightseeing at Baalbek. In addition to filling the tank, I had bought several extra containers of gasoline. I filled my two large canvas *chagals* with water and purchased two new extra tyres. Finally, I secured everything both inside and outside the car with plenty of rope, and felt confident Zobeida would pass any police inspection.

The military depot was only a few minutes' drive away. One could see that it had once been a caravanserai. On three sides the ancient walls were still standing, but the fourth had been pulled down to make extra space and the entrance gateway had also disappeared. For Allah knows how many centuries the serai had been the starting point of the east-bound caravan trade, and its walls had resounded to the rumbling and snarling of camels, the cacophony of lesser pack animals, and the shouts and curses of the caravan folk.

Now it seemed the old masonry must be shaken to its foundations by the thunder of the thousands of horsepower, as trucks and cars of every description warmed up their engines for the start. By a fantastic stretch of the imagination the scene resembled some gargantuan meet of hounds.

But I had no time for daydreaming. A couple of policemen, one of them a sergeant, strolled over and politely demanded to see my papers. They then made a quick inspection of the car.

They passed Zobeida as roadworthy, and the sergeant had just told me I was free to go when another policeman came up, followed by an Arab couple, evidently man and wife. After a few hurried words with his colleague, the sergeant turned to me and explained that the couple were passengers in another car which had been found unfit for the journey. As I was travelling alone, they asked if I would graciously permit them to travel with me.

The request was difficult to refuse, though it called for a last-minute rearrangement of all my baggage. I piled my bulky bedding-roll onto the front seat beside me and shifted suitcases and camp equipment, leaving barely room for the two passengers to climb in. Fortunately they had little baggage of their own.

'*Ashkurek*,' the husband grunted his thanks, as he shoved and heaved and finally levered his corpulent wife into the far corner. It was quite an effort, for in addition to being bulky, the good woman was swathed from tip to toe in an Arab *burqa*, which made her look like a giant cocoon, and she seemed very sensitive about not showing even a glimpse of her legs and feet.

'*Bism'illah*!' I replied. 'In the name of Allah.'

The sergeant gave me a polite salute.

The unseen master of this monstrous pack must have given the word to move off, for there was a grinding and clashing of gears and in a reeking ferment of diesel oil, gasoline fumes, camel-dung and the dust of ages, the whole diabolic assembly moved out of the serai.

The giant Nairn coach and several satellite vehicles had already gone. I followed modestly in line, realising with a sense of inferiority that Zobeida was the smallest, the lowest-powered and the lowest-priced vehicle in the whole caravan. Minutes later, with horns blaring out an ear-splitting tally-ho, we were careering up the coast road at well over forty miles per hour, with visibility ahead practically nil as we drove into the choking dust stirred up by the leading cars.

We had started in close line ahead, but gradually thinned out until I had about a quarter of a mile between me and my immediate leader's dust, and we settled down to a steady thirty-five miles per hour. This did not satisfy some of the impetuous boys behind and, with violent honking, every now and then one of them would go racing wildly past, to disappear into the cloud ahead.

The onward journey to Tripoli presented a constantly changing landscape of open scrub and heath-covered escarpments, reaching down like giant tentacles from the foothills of the Lebanon range away on our right. Every few miles we passed an ancient inn or caravanserai, its weathered walls and arched gateway a patchwork of varied masonry of every shape and colour, including delicately carved capitals and bases of columns, filched in the course of centuries from the ruins of pagan temples. Here and there, overgrown with clumps of pink and white oleander, a solitary archway or the posts and lintels of a massive gateway marked the site of some imposing structure long since disappeared.

Occasionally a Roman milestone would conjure up a momentary vision of foot-sore legionnaires, sweating in their burnished metal trappings and cursing the long dusty miles between them and Berytus.

This highway had been intended for men and animals, not for mechanised chariots driven by speed-crazy Jehus racing to perdition. Every so often, through the choking dust, I glimpsed young lads with donkeys cowering in the bushes by the roadside. If the ghosts of the legionnaires now scurried out of our way, the last laugh may still be theirs. Motor transport is a transient thing, and one day, if there remain any human survivors from our scientific 'progress', men with bows and arrows may tell their children of ghostly horseless chariots careering madly along the ancient coastal highway.

The convoy made a brief halt at Tripoli, and I climbed stiffly from the car. In a square lightly shaded by jacaranda trees, I sat down at a small café with rough wooden tables and benches outside, and ordered coffee, eggs and native bread. A friendly Arab truck-driver came and sat down beside me. He wore traditional head-dress, but the rest of his clothing was western, and he had on brightly coloured socks and sharply pointed yellow shoes. He addressed me politely in French, saying his name was Ahmed, and that Nairn's manager had told him to make himself known to me and to give me any assistance I needed. He ordered coffee and bread for himself. He was a handsome young man and looked intelligent.

There was little movement in the square save for a string of about a dozen camels, tied nose to tail, which shuffled haughtily by, led by a fat man riding a donkey. He sat eastern fashion astride the stern-end of his mount, where the tail connects with the spine. The little brute's legs were bending under his weight and the rider's feet dangled within an inch of the ground. The camels were laden with sawn-up trunks and branches of trees.

Ahmed pointed to the camels. 'You see what they're carrying? Those are mulberry trees . . . or at least they were. For many centuries this country has been famous for the production of beautiful silk. There you see the last of it. Imported Japanese silks and rayons have killed the industry. No use to keep silkworms any more, therefore no further need to cultivate the mulberry trees. The silkworms are gone and there go the trees—to Beirut for firewood.'

Ahmed asked me how Zobeida had been behaving. I told him I'd had no trouble so far, but was keeping my fingers crossed. I said she looked a trifle small for a trip like this, compared with all the other powerful monsters.

He laughed. 'It's not always the big ones that get through.' Then he said, 'You have some passengers, I see.'

My eyes followed his and I saw my Arab fellow-traveller climb stiffly from the car. His wife did not attempt to follow him.

'Uh-uh!' Ahmed exclaimed, and added in an undertone, 'Excuse me, but is he a friend of yours?'

'Not at all,' I said, and explained the circumstances. 'Why do you ask?'

'Oh, nothing, I just wondered if they were friends travelling with you.' He casually changed the subject, but I noticed that he kept his eyes on the Arab, who had lit a cigarette and stood by the car chatting with his wife.

'Well, time to be leaving.' Ahmed drank up his coffee and rose to his feet. 'Next stop Homs, but only a short one. *Insh'allah*, we reach Palmyra just before sundown. See you there. *Bon voyage*.'

From Tripoli the road ran for the first few miles through a continuous belt of orchards and cultivation. Then it left the coast, and ahead stretched a treeless sunbaked wilderness of stark black basalt rock.

There is something malevolent about basalt. It absorbs the solar rays and radiates them again with such burning intensity that one might suppose it had never completely cooled from its original volcanic boiling. It is merciless to man and beast, and brutal to rubber tyres. The going was not made any easier by numerous dry rocky water-courses, which slowed one's progress and had to be crossed with caution. Here and there, traces of weathered masonry reminded one that this was an ancient land saturated with history. We crossed the river Orontes and a couple of miles beyond it a collection of dusty overladen trucks and cars told me that this was Homs.

True to ancient tradition, the convoy had halted at the entrance to a caravanserai. The sun was right overhead and there was no shade. Many of the passengers climbed out to stretch their limbs or drink coffee and take a pull at a hookah. The drivers carried empty kerosene tins to a nearby well, filled them and replenished their radiators. I followed their example. Half the water in Zobeida's radiator had boiled away, but the oil level was satisfactory. I filled up the fuel tank from the reserve and inspected the tyres. I was prepared to find them badly cut, but they had not suffered too much from the grinding trek across the rough basalt. There would be a further stretch of this on the next stage, and then the desert.

No time to stroll around Homs, but from the outside it

looked shabby and uninspiring. The caravanserai and such other buildings as were visible seemed to be constructed mainly of basalt. This gave the place a gloomy and forbidding appearance, while everything that was not black seemed white hot in the seething rays of the sun.

Homs is the ancient Emesa. It was difficult to believe there could be a real lake in this parched wilderness of volcanic rock. Imaginary lakes there were a-plenty. Each way one looked, the mirage turned the landscape into quivering sheets of water. But somewhere, not many miles from the town, there must be real water, the Lake of Homs, famous not only as being the most ancient artificial reservoir of its size in the world, but also as being the site of the decisive battle of Emesa, in which the Roman legions under Aurelian routed the desert troops of Palmyra's Queen Zenobia, in the third century.

Homs . . . Emesa . . . the two names seemed to mingle in my ears with the dull hum of the motor, while the rhythm was punctuated by bumps, as we took a dried-up water-channel in our stride and straddled a rounded outcrop that would have eviscerated any low-strung city car.

I had begun to bless Zobeida's extra high clearance, but I was also learning not to overestimate it. Basalt is dangerous stuff and it would be foolish to take anything for granted with a light car like this one. Many of the other drivers now began to forge ahead of me, honking their horns derisively (I thought) as they swept past in a cloud of gritty dust.

I didn't blame them. Who was I to hold up these sons of the desert in their own terrain? They knew the road and its hazards, and they knew their cars. They were desert-tested. Besides, in most cases the cars were not their own. So *maleesh*!

From high overhead the sun was now working slowly to the rear as we continued to head due east. The glare on the barren landscape became less violent as the afternoon wore on, and the character of the terrain gradually changed. The plain now became flatter and broader, the basalt outcrops fewer, driving easier. But there was still no tree or bush or patch of verdure for the eye to rest upon. The air seemed even more oppressive, for the afternoon is the hottest part of the day. Above the surface of the ground the over-heated atmosphere danced and sizzled and the track ahead appeared to float in a constant sea of illusion.

I became drowsy as the hours passed and my thoughts began to wander. When one reaches this stage it is wisdom to halt the car awhile and get out and stretch one's legs. But I kept on driving.

Homs—Emesa—Zenobia—Palmyra! Yes, the battle must have been fought somewhere in that Allah-forsaken wilderness that now lay behind me. For a moment I let my gaze roam round the landscape. I pictured the glint of sunlight on the brazen trappings of the legions. It would have been visible many miles away and the distorting mirage probably made it appear even more terrifying. What had Zenobia thought as she first sighted that array of shining metal in the distance, and saw the solid lines of armour, the glittering spears and the cloud of dust rolling across the plain, kicked up by the hooves and chariot wheels of Aurelian's army? She must have realised in that moment that the day was lost.

I felt sorry for the Queen, surrounded by her obsequious ministers and yes-men. Many of them probably slunk away while there was still time. But Zenobia's desert horsemen were staunch, and must have put up a good fight. The scene became more vivid, until I could almost hear the blare of Roman trumpets, when the car gave a violent lurch which nearly flung me against the windscreen.

It brought me with a start back to the present day. It was nothing much, merely a rocky depression in the road, but rather deeper than most. It might have been serious, a broken spring or fractured axle, but I was lucky and no harm was done. It was a warning. No more daydreaming until we reached Palmyra.

We entered a range of hills by a narrow valley. We were in the Vale of Tombs. On either side were rectangular tower-like structures, rising up for two, three or four storeys to a height of sixty or seventy feet. Many of them looked like frontier watch-towers. I must have passed at least a hundred of these burial towers of wealthy Palmyrene families and felt tempted to stop and have a closer look, but evening was approaching, so I drove on.

Minutes later the hills opened out. The track, which was the ancient caravan route, emerged from the Vale of Tombs onto the open plain. Immediately ahead, and spreading out over the desert, was Palmyra itself, a vision of tawny golden colonnades extending from one central massive pile of the great temple of Bel, the sun god.

I had not thought to see anything so spectacular as the scene which now lay before me. I had expected a ruined city. Ancient ruins, wherever they may be located, always seem to possess certain features in common. But Palmyra was different. Here, except around the base of the temple itself, there was no confusion of tumbled masonry, no disorderly collection of decapitated columns, none of the piles of rubble which mark the ravages of earthquake or invader. Here there were far-reaching colonnades of marble pillars and archways standing intact and erect in their original alignment. The first impression was of a well-planned city which the builders, for some reason or other, had never completed.

There was no suggestion of violence. Here the enemy had been gradual decay. As the population had decreased or moved away, the desert had stepped in and cleaned up. The result was a scene of graceful beauty rather than chaotic grandeur.

The sun was just dipping behind the Vale of Tombs. A glorious desert sunset was in the making, throwing up the great parade of columns in vivid contrast to the drab background of the surrounding plain. From a deep yellow, which enhanced the rich texture of their stonework, the columns flushed to rose pink, while their shadows reached out like elongated purple fingers into the boundless sea of sand.

Most of the motley collection of cars and trucks were already halted inside the straggling compound of a crumbling caravanserai, but I sighted a more modern building a short distance away, with a number of military vehicles standing outside it. I prepared to make for it, thereby provoking a sudden and heated protest from my male Arab passenger.

At the same moment a couple of police officers halted me, then motioned me to drive on and park at the side of the modern building, which, I now saw, had a board at the entrance with the single word 'Hotel' painted on it.

As I climbed stiffly from the car, I saw my Tripoli acquaintance, Ahmed, hovering in the background, and sensed that something might be in the wind. It was. One police officer addressed me courteously and suggested I stay the night in the hotel. Meanwhile he wished to speak with my Arab passengers.

I picked up my camera and small overnight bag and made for the hotel entrance. As I reached it, I glanced back and saw my two passengers clamber slowly from the car. The policeman said something to them and they all walked away together, the fat woman in her *burqa* looking more like an oversize cocoon than ever. What big feet these Arab women have, I thought.

As soon as I had arranged for a room and had my baggage carried in, I hurried out to see what I could of the ruined city. Alas, there is no twilight in these latitudes and nothing was left of the sunset but a ruddy afterglow which vanished within minutes. There was no moon, but starlight took over where the sunset left off and there was no real darkness.

The night was still, save for an occasional cool gust which came whispering through the ruins. The whole atmosphere seemed haunted by the ghosts of the past, and the Arabs have a legend that the spirit of an ancient Queen can be seen on moonlit nights among the deserted columns.

The desert half-light plays lively tricks with the eyesight, let alone the imagination. I seated myself on a block of marble and idly watched the shadows as they danced across the façade of the temple, projected as in a giant shadow-show by the flickering cook-fires in the caravanserai. It required little imagination to see in them the shades of the ancient sculptors, craftsmen and masons who had built the great temple to the glory of their desert deity. And, following them in an age-long pageant and cavalcade, the city notables and merchant princes, the citizens and caravan folk, and the Queen, Zenobia herself, followed by the loyal desert warriors, lightly armed but superbly mounted, who from devotion to a beloved mistress died fighting the might of Imperial Rome.

It was getting late when at last I went indoors. The cookfires had gone out, and the bedlam of voices from the caravanserai had died to a subdued murmur. From the Arab village behind the temple walls came the muffled notes of some primitive flute. It was a melancholy, eerie sound. I shivered, as a chilly gust came wafting across the desert. It was the signal to go to bed.

It was difficult not to think about Zenobia. Her spirit seemed to pervade the atmosphere . . .

Palmyra, or Tadmor as it was called in biblical times, started as an obscure village in the heart of the desert. But it had three great assets; it had water, it lay on a main caravan route, and it happened to lie also in a central position between two great rival powers—Rome and Parthia.

As the bitter struggle between the two rival empires developed, the people of Tadmor saw the great advantages in remaining neutral and maintaining friendly relations with both warring powers. While the two giants dissipated their treasure and manpower in war, little Tadmor collected the pickings and waxed rich.

With their newly acquired wealth, the Tadmorians began to take an interest in things outside their own immediate bailiwick. The power of Rome was now in the ascendant and it became fashionable to have their children educated in the Imperial capital. Wealthy Tadmorians began to cut a figure in Roman society, and in the third century AD Odenathus, the ruling prince of Tadmor, attained great political power and prestige. Besides holding a seat in the Roman senate, he earned the gratitude of the Imperial Government by his efforts to strengthen Roman influence in the turbulent desert areas of what today is known as Kurdistan. The Romans found the Kurds a tough nut to crack and today, seventeen centuries later, the tribes in that area are still far from being pacified.

As a reward for this outstanding service, the Emperor Gallienus took the unusual step of conferring upon Odenathus the title of Co-Emperor. Shortly afterwards Odenathus headed a political mission to Parthia and there he was unfortunate enough to get himself assassinated.

His widow, Zenobia, was an ambitious young lady. She promptly assumed the leadership of her people and became one of the outstanding female characters of Asian history. When the Emperor Gallienus died, and signs of decadence were seen in Rome, Zenobia, sitting in her remote but prosperous city in the heart of the desert, began to dream an ambitious dream of empire.

It was not a desire for personal power that impelled her, so much as a yearning to build up a royal inheritance for her son Vallabathus. And the story is all the more pathetic because the wretched youth turned out a terrible disappointment.

Also the Queen was very poorly served by her counsellors. She would hear their reports of Roman defeats, of growing Roman weakness, and would review and compare her own troops of desert warriors. There was nothing decadent about them. They were fine fighting material, and man for man the equal of any legionaries. But what the Queen's counsellors failed to point out was her lack of reserves. The Romans had enormous reserves of trained soldiery to draw upon, while the Queen had no extra manpower in her sparsely populated desert domains.

If she considered this problem at all, Zenobia did not allow it to deter her. She put herself at the head of her troops and marched on Egypt. The Egyptians were defeated, and one success followed another until within four years she had extended her dominions from the Nile Valley to the highlands of Asia Minor.

It was an astonishing achievement, and who knows where it might have ended. But Zenobia's successes now began to alarm Rome, whose nerves were none too steady. The thought of a political rival building up on the eastern borders of their Empire sent shivers down their patrician backs. The last straw came when Zenobia issued coins bearing the impression of her head alone. Had she linked her graceful profile with that of the Emperor she might still have got away with it, but this was too much. Her vain little gesture convinced the Romans that the time had come to take Zenobia down a peg or two. Aurelian assembled his legions and marched into the desert against her.

The armies met on the basalt plain near Emesa, and the outcome was never in doubt. Aurelian, impressed by the beauty and bravery of the Queen, offered her generous terms of surrender, but Zenobia was smarting with shame and injured pride. She scorned Aurelian's offer. She fled towards the Tigris, was captured, and Aurelian carted her off to Rome to grace his triumph.

But the Romans knew how to respect courage, especially in a lovely woman, and Zenobia spent the rest of her days in honourable retirement in a villa on the Appian Way.

As for Tadmor, from a royal city it became a Roman garrison town. It remained an important military centre on the Empire's eastern frontier, but apart from its strategic value it lost all political and economic significance.

When the final decline of Roman power set in, Palmyra, as it came to be called, remained completely isolated from the West. In due course the Moslem wave engulfed it, but so long as caravans continued to use the desert route it still enjoyed a certain degree of prosperity. Then gradually, as the gloom of insecurity spread across the land, the caravan traffic dwindled, and Palmyra sank to the level of an Arab village, just a collection of miserable huts clustered around the ruins of the ancient temple.

And that is how I found it. Today, the ruined temple and the wealth of marble columns are all that remains of Palmyra's former splendour, while the villagers, ignorant of the city's early history, babble incoherently of desert *djinn* and the ghost of a lovely lady with a circlet of gold on her head, wandering mournfully by night among the deserted colonnades.

Chapter 3

PALMYRA TO BAGHDAD

Next morning, Ahmed greeted me as I completed loading the baggage on the car in readiness for an early start. There was no sign of my Arab passengers.

'You're well rid of them,' Ahmed said cheerfully. 'Today you'll travel light, and much faster.'

'What happened to them?' I asked.

He grinned. 'The police are holding them. I knew the man was no good when I first spotted him, and I tipped off the police at Tripoli.'

'And what about his wife?'

'His wife?' He laughed. 'That's a real joke, that is. It wasn't a woman at all. It was a man dressed in a *burqa*. Mohamed Salih's his name. The police were looking for him everywhere; in fact he's very high on their "Wanted" list. And, in addition, when they searched him they found a lot of contraband gold on him.'

'But it was the police who passed him on to me in the first place.'

'I know, and that's the biggest part of the joke. That sergeant in Beirut will never hear the last of this.'

'Any tips for the road?' I asked when Ahmed had finished laughing.

'No, it's all straightforward, and the going's quite good to Ramadieh, unless we hit a dust-storm. They've been having rather a lot of them recently. If one does start blowing up, keep going as long as you can see the car ahead, but stop as soon as you lose sight of it. Whatever you do, don't drive blind through a dust-storm, because once you're off the track and your wheel tracks get buried, you may never be picked up. Anyway, good luck, and see you in Baghdad.'

It was a pleasure, after the long ordeal over the basalt, to be able to drive steadily ahead for long stretches at a good speed. The only disconcerting feature was the constant rattle and banging as loose flints and pebbles were projected against the axle and undercarriage. They hit with such resounding force that I feared they might pierce the fuel tank.

The convoy, about forty vehicles in all, began to stretch out again, and soon the leading cars were mere clouds of dust on the horizon. Several raced past me, bombarding Zobeida with flying gravel as they passed. I felt maliciously happy when I later passed several of them stalled with engine trouble.

As the morning wore on, the sun blazed down from a torrid cloudless sky and the temperature soared. Away to the north-west there was a dark smudge on the horizon. I thought of dust-storms and remembered Ahmed's warning not to lose sight of the car in front. At this point the vehicle ahead of me was a light truck. I lessened the distance between us to about one hundred metres and aimed to keep it like that.

Soon, there was no doubt about the dark smudge; in a matter of a few minutes it had spread over that entire quarter of the sky. For a short while I thought the dust-storm might miss us, but in another ten minutes it had stretched itself right over the track ahead and was bearing down upon us with surprising speed. A few more minutes and half the sky was enveloped in a black impenetrable shroud. The sun was already obscured and it began to get dark. I pushed forward to within twenty metres of the truck ahead. I could see that it had an Arab driver, with a couple of companions on the seat beside him. None of them seemed at all perturbed by the great opaque mass bearing rapidly down upon them. I could feel the wind now, and the first dust cloud hit my windshield and peppered it with flying grit and pebbles.

The truck was still moving, but its pace had slackened. I slowed accordingly and reduced the distance to ten paces. In another couple of minutes I could barely distinguish its dark shape looming out of the dense greyness. I was now a bare two metres behind it, and at any other time or place would have been eating its dust, instead of which it was shielding me from the frontal brunt of the storm.

I expected the truck's driver to stop, but he kept going. I hoped he knew what he was doing, for I knew he had no other vehicle immediately ahead of him. I switched on my headlights, but they made no impression on the dense curtain of sand and dust. Then I sounded my horn, but those in the truck could never hear it above the noise of their own engine, plus the roar of the wind and the violent pounding of sand and gravel on the windscreen and body of the truck. I was sure that if I let that vehicle out of my sight for one moment, it would vanish and I would never see it again. And likewise, nobody might see me again.

After a few more minutes of this blind creeping through blackness—minutes which seemed interminably long—the truck crawled to a stop and I promptly did the same. For nearly half an hour the storm continued without slackening. I tried to remember what I had read about these desert dust-storms, and how long they might be expected to last, and estimated that I had enough food and water for a week or ten days if necessary.

At last the wind began to slacken, the cannonading became less violent and the gloom less dense. Soon it was daylight again. Three figures climbed down from the truck and I also got out of the car. The Arabs came up and began chatting. The driver of the truck spoke English, and we discussed the situation. We scanned the horizon ahead, but saw no sign of any cars, nor were any visible behind us. My first impulse was to go back on our tracks, but there were no tracks. A powdery dust, like a coating of freshly fallen snow, had completely obliterated our wheelmarks. We might guess the general direction, but the Arab admitted that he had continued to drive blindly and might have veered on to a wrong bearing.

Why the devil hadn't the fool kept the car ahead of him in sight as I had done! But it was no use saying anything. He was evidently a city Arab and probably knew no more about the desert than I did. I lit a cigarette and sat down in the car to think the matter over and, if necessary, wait until something turned up. It seemed clear that somehow or other we, the truck and I, had strayed well off the convoy route. Question: How long would it be before we were missed, and when we were, would anybody come back to look for us?

The answer was that, at the best, it might be a good many hours, or possibly even days. I preferred not to think of it. Instead I got out my field-glasses and scanned the horizon. I picked out several widely scattered clouds of dust. Some were nothing more than dust-devils, but others, mere light coloured puffs against the darker background, were being kicked up by a group of gazelle careering across the open plain.

I swept the glasses round in a half-circle, and then I saw just what I was looking for—several motor vehicles moving in a line.

At that moment the sun came out and, with full visibility restored, one could not fail to see the cars. The Arabs also spotted them and clambered gleefully back into their truck as I started my engine and got quickly under way. Twenty minutes later I was back on course with a couple of cars ahead of me whose drivers appeared sure of their direction.

After driving steadily and monotonously for hours on end across the drab featureless plain, the sight of a river or a town is a welcome event. To come across both town and river together, as one does at Hit and Euphrates, is a matter for rejoicing, even though as a city there is nothing very striking about Hit, other than its name. It is just one of many Arab towns, and no less squalid and dirty than the rest of them.

Like most of the inhabited centres of this ancient land, Hit rises on a self-created eminence, composed entirely of the debris and rubbish accumulated during three score centuries of more or less continuous habitation. Archaeologists today are inclined to credit Jericho with being the world's most ancient continuously inhabited city, but Hit in the Land of the Two Rivers must be a close competitor.

Until the 1914–18 war brought in modern weapons and mechanised transport, conditions in this desert land had undergone little change. The tramp of armed forces was nothing new to Hit. For the best part of four thousand years the town had stood here overlooking the road of invasion and conquest. Empires rose and fell, fought and conquered or lost, marching and counter-marching along the desert highway beneath the sunbaked walls of Hit. From time to time an overwhelming tide of invasion would sweep down like an all-destroying river flood, as when the Mongol hordes descended and Baghdad and all the lesser cities were wiped out.

After a period of utter desolation a few survivors would creep back and, like a herd of antelope disturbed and scattered by the hunter, would gradually regroup. Then, upon the debris of the latest devastation, itself piled upon that of earlier destruction, a new city would arise a little higher above the plain than its predecessors. And life would continue as before.

Hit has been fortunate in having a permanent industry of its own—permanent in the sense that it has continued in operation since earliest biblical times. A bare three kilometres to the south-west of the town the ancient bitumen pits are still being worked, and the wind carries fumes from them far across the plain.

Ramadieh, next landmark on the road, is an uninspiring cluster of squalid dwellings with an outsize caravanserai. Soon, at Fallujeh, we crossed the swirling, muddy Euphrates by a shaky pontoon bridge, and then we were literally in Mesopotamia, the Land between the Two Rivers.

On all sides were the remains of ancient water channels, part of great irrigation systems which the invading Mongols amused themselves by destroying. As an act of large-scale sabotage they did a very thorough job. They were habitually big-time operators, and had no lack of experience. They were next destined to perform an equally thorough operation in the massacre of virtually the whole population of Baghdad and the destruction of the entire city.

The long tiring journey was now nearing its end. My thoughts turned to such luxuries as a cold drink, a bath and a good meal. I peered into the distance ahead for signs that I was approaching Baghdad. I expected to see ruined serais and remains of ancient buildings, such as had lain strewn throughout the regions nearer the Mediterranean. Then I remembered that in this country there is very little stone. The building medium, whether for Caliph's palace or Arab hovel, was brick—brick made of mud and straw, and sometimes only mud. For important buildings the bricks were kiln-baked, but for ordinary purposes they were just dried in the sun. The kiln-baked bricks were extraordinarily tough and long-lasting, but the sun-dried variety disintegrated when long exposed to sun and water. So I gave up looking for historic ruins, and instead kept my eye on the horizon ahead for the first glimpse of Baghdad itself.

Away to the left of the road, low down on the skyline, a yellowish glare resolved itself into two separate glittering domes. From their position at an angle to my route I realised that they marked the holy city of Qadhimein. Then after a while I sighted the glint of sunlight on another mosque, directly ahead of me. This could only be Baghdad.

I caught up with two cars of our convoy halted at a customs control post while a couple of uniformed officials examined their baggage. They were also inspecting the vehicles in a very thorough manner, even removing and looking inside the hub-caps. I learned later that they were searching for smuggled drugs and gold.

As I slowed to a halt, a third official came out from a barrack-like building with the Iraqi flag flying over it. He demanded and glanced at my passport, and seeing that I had no passengers he gave me a friendly grin and waved me on. Close ahead of me were other cars just moving off after a prolonged inspection, and I followed them into Baghdad.

A few tired-looking date-palms, their fronds thick with powdery grey dust, sprawled over a drab stretch of mud-coated wall. I drove past a succession of coffee-houses, from one of which came the raucous blare of canned native music. A handful of dazed patrons sat dreamily on rudely made wooden chairs, silent and motionless, save for the languid movement of an arm, as its owner took a leisurely pull at the inevitable *naghileh.* The only bright spots relieving the general air of shabbiness were the red or blue chequered head-cloths of the somnolent Arabs, and the glint of golden sunshine on the multi-coloured tiled dome of the nearby mosque.

Such were my first impressions of the city of Harun-ar-Rashid.

A genial-looking Englishman now accosted me by name and introduced himself as Nairn's manager. He told me he had reserved me a room at the Maude Hotel. 'The only fit place to stay in,' he said. 'The food varies. Sometimes it's good, other times it's unbelievably bad. They've recently engaged a new chef and at present it's reasonably good.'

'Fine,' I said, 'I can certainly do with a good meal. What's the accommodation like?'

'Well,' he said, a little cautiously, 'it's the best in Baghdad, and I've booked you one of the rooms facing the river, they're the coolest. The hotel's only just round the corner. I suggest you go and register straight away, and I'll tell our men to carry up your kit.'

Chapter 4

BAGHDAD

Architecturally, the Maude Hotel was an attempted compromise between East and West. One escaped from the glaring sunlight through a dark passage-way, leading into a courtyard or quadrangle surrounded by drab buildings of coffee-coloured brick.

I filled up the form at the reception desk, and the clerk, who spoke a little English, took down from its hook an oversize rusty iron key, which once upon a time might have hung from the waistband of Harun-ar-Rashid's chief eunuch. He handed the key to a diminutive Arab bell-hop, who led me down a flight of brick stairs into what appeared to be a basement, until I noticed that both the dining-room and the lounge were down there. I soon learned that in the more substantial Baghdadi houses the living-quarters are constructed well below ground level. These rooms are known as the *sardabeh*, or cool cellars, and fully justify their name, for the enervating outside heat never penetrates down there, though some form of flue ventilation must exist, for the air remains reasonably fresh.

From semi-darkness we emerged into brilliant daylight onto a broad tree-lined terrace facing the swirling chocolate-coloured waters of the Tigris and giving a view of the opposite bank of the river. This was built up with a continuous line of old wooden buildings, bizarre and picturesque, with their crazy balconies and mysterious lattice windows. Their paint-work, originally in crude blues and reds and greens, had faded with age into delicate pastels. The scene must have delighted many artists, and the balconies, precariously over-hanging the fast-flowing current, conjured up visions of Old Baghdad and the *Thousand and One Nights*.

From the hotel terrace, short wooden stairways gave access to the front row of bedrooms. The bell-hop led me up one of these, and paused to unlock the door of my room. It was a massive wooden affair of primitive appearance, secured with a battered iron lock and heavy metal bolt. The *walad* (it means 'boy', but sounds better in the vernacular), like a dwarf seneschal of some crusader castle or warden of a donjon, now brought the big rusty key into action. With a little struggle he managed to edge it into the lock, and with a two-handed effort succeeded in turning it. He pushed back the ponderous bolt, and the heavy door swung slowly open, creaking on its hinges as though in protest at being disturbed.

I quite expected to find myself in medieval surroundings and if the furnishings of the room were not genuinely antique, they were at least gothic in their primitive simplicity. Two iron bedsteads, a plain wooden table and chairs, were set off by an unusually fine Persian rug stretched across the bare wooden boarding of the floor. An electric ceiling fan with three large blades added a modern touch. The *walad* pushed the switch and slowly, reluctantly, the blades began to rotate. Seeming surprised, but with evident relief, the *walad* exclaimed 'W'Allah! it works!'

A number of hornets had their nests suspended from the ceiling. Would the fan disturb them I wondered, and if so would they vent their annoyance on it or on me? But the breeze from the slowly rotating blades was so gentle and the ceiling so high, I decided to ignore the hornets and hoped they would reciprocate.

Adjoining the bedroom was the bathroom. By now I was prepared for anything. There was a chipped enamel wash-basin, a soap-dish with a thin tablet of bright pink highly scented soap, evidently left by the last occupant, a galvanised iron hip-bath, and the inevitable wooden 'thunder-box'. Its lid was open to show that it was empty and ready for service, and on the upper edge of the lid where it rested against the wall, a large scorpion was airing itself. I pointed this out to the *walad*, who exclaimed 'W'Allah!', promptly drew a piece of cloth from the folds of his *galabieh*, and quickly disposed of the creature. I had a good look round, but apart from a few hornet cells, I saw no more noxious animal life.

I asked about a bath. One particular *walad*, I was told, was responsible solely for the water arrangements, and would bring me my bath water, hot or tepid, (it was never cold), one pitcherful at a time. The thunder-box side of the business, I was glad to learn, was the sole responsibility of another *walad*.

Despite the absence of such refinements as electric bells, there was no difficulty about service. All I had to do was to step to the open door and bawl at the top of my voice '*walad!*' Sooner or later, and as I learned by experience it was usually later, a *walad* would appear from the labyrinthine depths of the hotel. Rarely would he be the particular one I wanted, but if not he would disappear again and eventually the right one would be found and the service performed without further delay.

My immediate need now was to get the bath filled up. That accomplished, I dug out from my baggage fresh underlinen and a badly creased tropical suit. Then, having bathed and dressed, my thoughts turned to the prospect of food.

Here, I suffered a setback. The clerk in the office informed me that dinner would be served punctually at 7.00 P.M., and the tone of voice clearly intimated that it would be less than useless expecting it one minute earlier, so I stifled my hunger and sauntered out onto the terrace which overlooked the river.

The sun was already nearing the horizon, its rays diffused by a thick curtain of desert dust which blanketed the western sky and caused it to glow a violent crimson, like the reflection from some distant forest fire. Immediately in front and below me flowed the Tigris. In daytime it is a broad expanse of brown muddy water, impressive in its width and massive volume, but with no pretence to beauty. This was how it had appeared to me earlier that afternoon. But now, reflecting the sunset, it appeared a lurid crimson torrent, vividly suggesting a river of blood.

It was pleasantly cool, though the gravel on the terrace

radiated the stored-up daytime heat. I seated myself on a wooden bench. The sound of the river lapping the bank had a soporific effect, and I felt a growing drowsiness after the long desert journey. I let my imagination play with visions of the city's glamorous past.

From over the water I heard the deep clanging of a camel-bell, and I could just discern a string of shadowy, long-legged shapes silhouetted against the fiery red background of the sky, as they shuffled their way across the nearby bridge. Accompanying the notes of the leading animal's bell came the sound of the camel-man's wavering monotonous chant, that only an Arab can sing and only a camel can understand. Centuries ago . . . when Baghdad was just a few mud huts, clustered on the banks of a desolate muddy river . . .

It had been the great El Mansur, the second Abbasid Caliph, who had founded the city in AD 763. During the following five centuries it remained the capital of Islam and as such flourished exceedingly.

It reached a peak of prosperity and magnificence under the rule of the Caliph Harun-ar-Rashid, the famous sleepless nightwalker of the *Arabian Nights*. All the skill of the Moslem world went into the designing of its mosques and palaces. All the riches of the Orient flowed into the bulging caravanserais and store-houses. The clanging of camel-bells must have been unceasing in those days, as the desert caravans followed in steady succession along the ancient trade routes, bringing in a constant flood of merchandise—silks from Cathay, carpets from Iran, gems and gold cloth from Hindustan, myrrh, frankincense and gums from Arabia, gold, ivory and pearls from Africa.

El Mansur had founded the city, but Harun-ar-Rashid converted it into a work of art and beauty, and more important still into a centre of learning and culture that had no equal in his day. He established schools and universities whose fame attracted students and teachers from all over the civilised world, East and West, and his name remains legendary to this day.

For his palaces and public buildings Harun drew upon the limitless store of brickwork from the ruins of Babylon and Borsippa, with marble columns from Palmyra, hundreds of kilometres away across the desert. Great stone-vaulted bazaars formed a giant emporium for the wealth of merchandise culled from the marts of three continents.

Across the river, reaching out over a wide expanse, were the royal precincts, surrounding the great marble and basalt palace, in which the Commander of the Faithful maintained the most magnificent court in the entire Orient. Screened off by alabaster lattice-work was the seraglio. Here lived a select community of the finest and most ravishing women that money could buy: fair-skinned *houris* from Circassia, sloe-eyed damsels from Kashmir, vivacious young maidens from the Kurdish hills, languid Indian ladies and slant-eyed Mongol princesses, captured from conquered territories, taken as tribute, received as presents, or simply purchased from the latest incoming slave train.

Giant negro eunuchs, fattened to the highest degree of perfection and wielding broad-bladed scimitars, guarded the doors to all this priceless human treasure.

Behind the river, the fringe of date-palms stood out like a border of black lace against the darkening sky. Along the river bank the outlines of old houses with their wooden balconies overhanging the water were still discernible, although their faded colours were now a uniform shade of grey. With the *Arabian Nights* still in my mind, I thought how very convenient those balconies must have been for the disposal of refuse, of unwanted chattels and superfluous concubines. A push, a faint splash and unlike Scheherazade, the Tigris tells no tales.

The effect of the sunset was now fading, but the water still reflected the deep red glow. So very like blood! Thus it must have looked during those terrible days in AD 1258, when the Mongol hordes of Hulagu came sweeping over the desert to fall upon the defenceless city. They were methodical savages. They first destroyed the vast and intricate irrigation system, thereby cutting off the water supply. Then they attacked the city. They spared neither man, woman nor child, but sacked and looted, raped and murdered until the devastation was complete.

All the handiwork of Harun and his successors, together with the entire population, went up in the smoke of one gigantic funeral pyre.

All that was left to mark the site of the city of the Great Insomniac, of his wife Zobeida, of Scheherazade and of the lovely concubines was a vast area of smouldering ruins. Baghdad had gone the way of Nineveh and Babylon.

Passing through the bar on my way to the dining-room, I came across Nairn's manager. He was just leaving, but stayed for a quick drink and a chat. He advised me strongly not to venture into Iran without a Persian servant, or better still a man with some knowledge of cars, who could be helpful in an emergency. He felt sure that a small announcement in the local newspaper would produce some applicants. I felt his advice was sound, and resolved to act upon it.

There was an Englishman at the next table in the dining-room. It was not quite seven, and dinner was not yet served. We got into a casual chat over our whiskies and sodas, but it was not an exciting conversation.

After eyeing me cautiously for a few moments, and doubtless noting my crushed suit, he broke the ice:

'Just arrived by convoy?'

'Yes.'

'Staying long?'

'Few days. Going on to Iran.'

'By car?'

'Yes.'

'Been up there before?'

'Not this side of the country.'

'Speak the lingo?'

'Yes.'

'Got a servant, I suppose?'

'No. Matter of fact, I haven't.'

'Mean you're driving up there all alone?'

'That's about it.'

He shook his head. 'Wouldn't if I were you. I'd get a servant.'

'I thought of that, but decided to wait till I got up there. No good taking an Arab. Language and all that.'

'Baghdad's full of Iranis. Should be no difficulty finding one who knows about cars. He'd be a great help to you.'

'Perhaps you're right.'

'You'd be wise. A small ad in the *Baghdad Times* would be almost certain to fetch somebody.'

At this point dinner arrived and the conversation lapsed.

Next morning after breakfast I found my way round to the office of the English-language newspaper and placed the following announcement: 'Wanted. Irani mechanic, able to drive car and prepared to travel in Iran. Good references required. Apply . . .'

I resolved to postpone my departure a day or two in order to deal with possible applicants. This would give me an opportunity to have a look around Baghdad, also I welcomed the chance to get some exercise after the long days sitting cramped in the car. There was now something approaching a feeling of spring in the air; the mornings and evenings were agreeably cool, while the night temperature dropped rapidly after sundown.

I was not so much interested in the bazaars of Baghdad as I was in seeing what, if any, vestiges still remained of the original city of the Caliphs. The bazaars themselves followed the pattern of most other Middle-Eastern cities, but there was one section, the Street of the Amarah Silverworkers, which had a distinctive character all its own.

Here, a community of black-bearded artisans hammered lustily on little anvils. A community is the proper name for them, since they are much more than a guild of craftsmen; they are a sect with a special religion peculiarly their own. In no other profession, unless it be in India, has the son so consistently and exclusively inherited and pursued the craft of his father, back through untold generations.

Over the first shop in the street, which was also the workshop, hung a painted wooden sign with the rather startling text 'John The Baptist Najeeb Amarah Silver-work'. Next door was another sign, 'John The Baptist Jameel', and so on down the street. These were not, as might at first be supposed, mere trade names, such as the Kashmiri merchants of Srinagar display to attract Western customers. All these black-bearded craftsmen claim descent from John the Baptist, and use the same praenomen. They all come from around Amarah in northern Iraq, and claim that city as their religious centre on the alleged grounds that it was the last resting place of John the Baptist. This, however, is an article of faith rather than factual history.

At this time there were estimated to be less than eight thousand members of this obscure sect, who described themselves as Sabaeans or Mandeans. Ethnologists dispute the traditional origin of the Amarah Sabaeans, though they credit them with an ancestry far more remote than the age of John the Baptist. Moreover, despite their professed reverence for the Baptist, apart from not being true Sabaeans, they are not even genuine Christians. They are said to be descendants of an obscure pagan people who, in the early days of militant Islam, sought successfully to evade forcible conversion by assuming the name of Sabaean and claiming to be, in common with Christians and Jews, 'people of the book'.

Whatever the truth of the matter, it cannot be denied that the Amarah Silversmiths are a very ancient sect, pursuing a very ancient craft. I watched John the Baptist Najeeb as he squatted by his little anvil and etched the outline of a bow-legged camel on a flattened sheet of silver. He dusted some antimony into the design, thrust it into the glowing charcoal embers of his miniature forge and, after cooling, burnished the surface with fine brick-dust. The tools he used were crude and primitive and could hardly have changed much since the days of John himself.

My search for relics of the City of the Caliphs was

unrewarding. I was shown a few sections of old wall and a portion of the entrance to a mosque that were said to be, and possibly were, remnants of buildings that had stood in the Abbasid capital, but actually I was able to locate only one single ancient monument that has some convincing claim to authenticity. This was the tomb of the Sitt Zobeida. Even so, how much of the present structure formed part of the original tomb is in doubt, but it seems to be generally accepted that beneath it did once lie the remains of Harun's favourite wife, Zobeida.

The Caliph himself was not buried in Baghdad. He died in the spring of AD 809 in Khorasan, and shares a mausoleum in Meshed with the Imam, Ali-al-Riza. It is an interesting thought that in this ancient land, where until recently women were still regarded as little more than chattels, of all the great mosques and palaces built by Harun-ar-Rashid to the glory of Allah and the Abbasids, one solitary mud-coloured tomb survives to preserve his memory—the grave of Zobeida, a woman!

Another link with the remote past, going back far beyond the Caliphate or even John the Baptist, are the ancient river-craft. I was particularly intrigued by the *gufas*, round coracle-type vessels, shaped like Indian *lotas*. They are made of goat- or sheepskin stretched over a wicker framework and water-proofed with an outer coating of pitch. As sole decoration, a few blue beads or cowrie shells set into the rim serve as talismans to ward off bad luck or the evil eye. The *gufas* probably originated in the upper reaches of the Tigris in the days of Noah. I stood and watched, fascinated, as one of these floating pudding-basins, carried by the current, came gliding downstream. It was laden to the brim with vegetables and was followed by another bearing a cargo of sheep and goats and by yet a third carrying human freight. These *gufas* must be extremely difficult to steer, although the Arab boatmen, born to the game, keep perfect control with one clumsy square oar and a minimum of visible effort. The most graceful craft on the river are the *maheilas*, with slender sloping mast and pointed bows. They too are clearly of antique design, and fit perfectly into the fascinating picture of the historic waterway.

The response to my advertisement was disappointing. Applicants were fewer than I had expected, and did not come anywhere near meeting my requirements.

For one thing, most of them were not Iranis, but Arabs. They did not even speak Persian. Of the few real Iranis who presented themselves, the first was an aged *Hadji*. He must have been at least seventy. He had a wizened face, twinkling eyes, a green turban, and a bright red henna-dyed beard.

He did not immediately explain his reason for calling on me, but the hotel clerk, evidently impressed by the visitor's age and venerable appearance, enhanced by the green turban of the *Hadji* (one who has made the pilgrimage to Mecca), sent him up to my room in charge of the pocket-sized bellhop. The youngster conducted him as far as my door, knocked, then slipped away leaving him on the mat as it were.

When I opened the door, the old gentleman saluted me gravely with a sedate motion of hand to forehead, but said not a word. Puzzled, but impressed by his dignified bearing, I motioned to him to enter. He seated himself on a chair, tucked his feet politely out of sight underneath his robe, and his hands into his broad sleeves, and for a few moments stared at me in silence. Then with true Persian politeness he enquired about my health. *Insh'allah*, I was well? I agreed that I was, and expressed the hope that, *insh'allah*, his own health was also good.

'*Alhamdulillah*,' he assured me that it was, and lapsed into silence. Still I waited patiently for him to unburden himself. I was on the point of suggesting that he might care for a coffee, when he murmured something about the *Ahkbar-i-Ingles*, the English newspaper, and only then did I realise what it was all about.

Once the ice was broken, he made himself quite clear. He understood I would be travelling up into Iran by car: would I give him a free ride as far as Hamadan, his home town?

I had to explain at length why, very regrettably, it would not be possible, and the old gentleman smilingly said it was of no consequence, but that he had never yet been in a motor-car and would have enjoyed the experience.

In the course of the morning three other applicants appeared. All claimed to have some acquaintance with motor-cars, but could produce no evidence in support of this. In any case they were only prepared to go with me as far as Tehran and practically admitted they were just trying to get a free ride. I was disappointed, because by this time I had heard more about the state of the less frequented roads in Iran, and everything I heard convinced me that to travel alone would be not only risky, but very foolish.

It was already evening, and I was just in the middle of the complicated operation of having my before-dinner bath. The water *walad* had so far brought only the first two pitcherfuls, and I had covered myself with a thick, rich lather of soap. There was a delay in the arrival of the third pitcher, and as I stood in two inches of tepid bath-water in all my naked glory, the door opened. For a moment, half blinded by the soap in my eyes, I thought it was the *walad*, but when the figure greeted me with '*Salaam aleikum, Agha!*' I had a shock. It was a complete stranger.

At that moment the *walad* returned with the water and with great presence of mind and dexterity he emptied the pitcher over me with one hand, while giving the intruder a push with the other. He let go a torrent of Arabic, while I hastily scraped myself free of soap. I dried myself quickly and, draped in a bath-robe, I received my visitor in the bedroom.

For a moment I could not think who he might be, but when he mumbled something about '*Baghdada Times*' I saw the light. Here was another applicant.

He was of medium height and build and, I guessed, in his middle thirties. He had regular features, black hair and eyebrows, and wore the usual round Persian hat. He told me his name was Abdul Samad, or just Abdul for short. His home was in Isfahan and he had originally come down to Baghdad to seek work. He had tried different jobs and the last one had been with a garage. He produced a much thumbed scrap of paper in support of this. I could barely decipher the name of the garage and accepted it for what it was worth. He said he knew the road as far as Isfahan quite well and was less well acquainted with the country as far as Shiraz. Beyond that he had never been and never wished to go. It was all *biaban*—a wild and desolate land. However, if Allah so willed, he would go with me to *akhir-i-dunya*, the end of the earth.

Being used to the flowery Persian idiom, I did not take this too literally, but accepted his assurance that he would help with the car and any other work within reason. As to terms, we agreed a monthly rate of pay, plus an extra allowance for the road, a bonus of one month's wages on termination of his service, and his travelling expenses back to Isfahan. He said his papers were in order, and he was prepared to leave at any time—next morning, if I wished.

I decided to take a chance, and engaged Abdul. I told him to settle whatever affairs he had and report to me the next afternoon. I quite expected him to request a cash advance on account, but he did not and I took this as a good omen. He agreed that it would be cold, very cold up in the mountains, but said he had everything he needed.

The next afternoon he turned up carrying bundle rolled up in an old rug, which he explained contained his warm clothing. This subsequently turned out to be a well-worn sheepskin kaftan, rather like the *posteens* worn by the Afghan caravan folk. He said he had purchased it from a Tabrizi who had come down on a pilgrimage and found the Baghdad climate too hot for that sort of clothing. We went through a practice drill of loading up Zobeida. I laid in a fresh supply of fuel and oil and everything was ready for the road.

The following morning we made an early start so as to cover the ninety-odd miles across the desert to the Iranian border before the heat of the day set in. I had expected to meet a fair amount of motor traffic on the way, for the road we were following was the ancient trade route which had linked with the Great Silk Road through Central Asia. But save for a few isolated trucks and cars within the outskirts of Baghdad, all we met were occasional strings of camels, pack-horses and mules.

I was surprised that for such a main highway there was no properly made road, only a dirt track tramped hard by generations of flat-footed camels and the foot of man. Though motor traffic had not been heavy, it had already carved out for itself two deep lines of wheel tracks, formed mainly in wet weather when the surface was soft and yielding.

I should mention that, as the result of British influence in Iraq, the rule of the road was 'keep to the left' as in England.

We were already approaching the frontier when we sighted a motor-car coming towards us across the open plain. It was travelling rapidly and raising a cloud of dust in its trail. We had the whole desert to pass in, but I kept instinctively to the left of the track. Meanwhile the oncoming driver kept to his right and continued to do so as the distance between us grew rapidly less. I naturally expected the other fellow to cross to the proper side, to his left, but he showed no sign of doing so, nor did he even reduce speed. All he did was to sound his horn violently. Was the fool blind or drunk or out of his senses? In a matter of seconds there would have been a head-on collision.

I wrenched the wheel over hard, and swerved out of the way in the very nick of time. I shouted at him, and he shouted back at me. I braked and pulled up, and he did the same. We both got out and walked towards each other. I saw he was a European.

'What the hell . . .' he began angrily in the unmistakable voice of an Englishman.

'Why the devil did you keep to the wrong side of the road?' I broke in.

'What d'you mean,' he retorted, 'it was you who were on the wrong side!'

A sudden thought struck me. 'What side of the road d'you keep in Iran?'

'The right-hand side, of course.'

'Well, now you're in Iraq, and here we keep to the left.'

He looked disconcerted for a moment, then broke into a loud laugh. 'Well, I'll be damned. Awfully sorry, old chap. My fault. I've been up in Tehran so long, I'd completely forgotten.'

'Just as well it happened down here,' I said, 'or I might have continued driving on my left all the way up into the Iranian hills.'

'You wouldn't be the first to crash down the mountainside. You'll see the wrecks of plenty of cars that did just that.'

We got back into our respective cars. 'Have a good trip.'

'Same to you.' And we parted, still laughing.

Chapter 5

IRAN FRONTIER TO KERMANSHAH

We passed the Iranian customs post without delay or difficulty and the friendly official advised us not to loiter on the road and to make sure of reaching Kermanshah before nightfall. He also insisted on my having an escort, and two *tufangchis*, or militiamen, were detailed to accompany me. They were dirty and bedraggled, they might easily have been bandits, and I was annoyed at having them forced upon me as passengers.

I protested I did not need an escort, for I suspected it was only a pretext to cadge a free ride. But the official shook his head. I must have an escort. It was an order.

'Is there any trouble on the road?' I asked, while Abdul helped the two *tufangchis* to squeeze themselves in behind the baggage.

'*Che arz kunam*, what petition may I make,' he replied with that delightfully vague and most frequently used of all Persian expressions. 'We have patrols out on the road and, *insh'allah*, if Allah wills, nothing will happen, but after sundown that is different.' He raised his eyebrows and sank his neck into his shoulders as much as to say, 'Well, what can you expect? This is not Europe; this is Kurdistan, and after all even a Kurd must live.'

Later, in Kermanshah, we learned that the official's concern for our safety had been justifiable. Only two days previously cars had been fired upon and passengers robbed, while a few days before that a whole party had been ambushed and several killed. Yes, indeed, the poor Kurds must live!

*

Now we were at last on Iranian soil, and the real journey was just beginning. Away ahead in the distance were lofty mountain ranges, and the road immediately began to rise. I regretted the extra weight of the escort, which meant so much more strain on Zobeida. I handed the *tufangchis* a few cigarettes, which they acknowledged gratefully, and they continued to smoke and chatter in subdued tones all the way to Kermanshah.

Abdul now produced his sheepskin kaftan and in it looked the typical bandit. He sat by my side in the front seat. I preferred to do the driving, especially on the more difficult parts of the road which lay ahead. It was well that I did, for later, on a perfectly level stretch, I changed places with him and let him take the wheel while I studied the map and made notes.

Two minutes later we were very nearly off the road and down the hillside. I grabbed the wheel just in time and took over again.

Abdul was apologetic. He was out of practice he said. Now, for the first time I asked him if he had had much driving experience.

'*Che arz kunam*,' he shrugged.

'Have you ever driven at all?' I persisted.

There was a brief pause. '*Nakhair, Agha*. No, sir, Never.'

'Then what did you do in the garage?'

'I worked as a cook.'

I consoled myself with the thought that it might be just as well to have a cook with me on a long journey, though I hesitated to probe into Abdul's culinary qualifications. Perhaps, after all, I would never have to put them to the test. And there still remained the job of looking after the baggage, an onerous business which I hated.

As a youngster about to go out East for the first time, I had learned that there were two conflicting schools of thought on this baggage question. One seasoned old traveller, a friend of my family, had told me: 'Now remember, my boy, on a long journey always carry as much as you can as far as you can, and stay with it as long as you can.'

I could quite see the advantage of that policy in countries with abundant cheap labour, or when travelling with camel-caravan or mule-train. But my faith in the old traveller's advice was shaken when an uncle, who had spent most of his military service in India, and had done a great deal of *shikar* and much original exploring, declared with some warmth: 'Damn nonsense. Don't you believe him. Take my advice; always travel as light as you can, and live off the country.'

On this present trip I had tried to strike a mean between the two schools. I had kept my cooking equipment, food supplies, bedding and clothing down to a practical minimum, and limited extras to little more than my typewriter and cameras, but the requirements of the car itself more than made up for this restraint. I had been warned in Baghdad that except in the larger cities I could never count on obtaining a refill of fuel or lubricant, and that to be safe I must carry a plentiful supply with me, including water for the radiator. Consequently, every inch of space both inside and outside the car was taken up with my reserve supplies.

All of these I put in the charge of Abdul, and made it his responsiblity to check each item every day and generally see to it that when we stopped anywhere the village ragamuffins did not pilfer things.

For the rest, Abdul just sat beside me and discoursed on the landscape, the people we passed on the road and many other things. I forgave him his lack of mechanical skill when I found him surprisingly well informed for a person of his station in life.

But what *was* his station in life? I asked myself. The very phrase seemed stilted and inappropriate out there in the wilds of Kurdistan. This was not India. There was no caste system. There were wealthy and poor, townspeople and country people, landowners and peasantry, plainsmen and hill-folk, villagers and nomads. In the cities there were merchants, shopkeepers, and religious dignitaries, *mullahs* and *muftis*, and so forth, and there were officials of every rank and degree.

But where a man like Abdul would fit into this social network, I had no idea. I had hired him as a mechanic, a handyman and general servant, and the question of his educational background had never occurred.

However, I began to see him in a new light as the journey progressed. It is often the little things that catch the attention and I was pleasantly surprised to find Abdul quite knowledgeable about birds and animals. At least he seemed to know the names of many of them, which is more than can be said of most town-dwellers, whether in Iran or elsewhere in Asia. Later I found that his knowledge of natural history was not as deep as his acquaintance with folklore, and if he knew the name of a bird or animal it was usually associated with some legend or tradition.

The first instance of this was a flight of storks. I was surprised to see them so early in the year. Abdul was quick to nudge me and point them out.

'See them, Agha. There go the pilgrims!'

'Pilgrims? What pilgrims?'

'Those birds, Agha, they are good birds.'

'I know they are good birds, but why pilgrims?' I had forgotten the popular name for stork.

'*Hadji lak-lak*, Agha,' and then he reminded me. 'The stork is a good bird because he is a good Moslem. He talks Arabic. He is always repeating "*lak*", which in Arabic means "to Thee", to Thee praise, to Thee glory. And he flies away and does the pilgrimage to Mecca every year.'

I looked at Abdul. His face was perfectly serious. No doubt at all that the stork was a *Hadji*.

'You are right, I always liked storks,' I said.

From Kasr-i-Shirin the road mounted steadily. Behind and below us the drab expanse of Mesopotamia lay shimmering in a haze of heat and dust. We had left the territory of one ancient empire and were ascending to the domains of another of equal antiquity. From the plains of the Two Rivers we were climbing in curving gradients to the higher level of the Iranian Plateau.

We were following one of the great highways of history. Along it, in the course of successive millennia, invading armies had marched down to attack the fertile lands of the great rivers, while others had fought their way up to overrun the uplands and the great plateau. While Darius maintained his summer capital at Ekbatana, there would have been a constant movement of armed forces along this road, and at least one of the great ruler's victorious campaigns has been commemorated in sculpture a few kilometres further up at Bisitun.

One could see that the road had once been in good condition, thanks to the British engineers who worked on it in 1918. But since then no repairs had been carried out. Frost and snow and heavy rains had worked havoc, and in places where the mountainside fell away precipitously the road had crumbled at the edges, leaving barely enough width of track for a car to pass. In such places very careful driving was called for, but not always observed, judging by the numerous remains of vehicles that lay crumpled and rusting at the bottom of the valley far below.

On the whole, Zobeida's performance had been satisfactory, especially considering the heavy load and two extra bodies, though for the last steep gradients up to the saddle known as Sar-i-Pul, I had to crawl in bottom gear. This was the highest point we had so far reached, though still stiffer climbs lay ahead.

We stopped at the top to have a look at the surrounding country. To the eye it all appeared barren and windswept, and not unlike portions of the Indian north-west frontier. These mountains were already part of Kurdistan, but of the Kurds themselves we had seen no sign.

At this point Abdul turned to me and asked, 'Is your Honour interested in ancient history?' The sudden question took me by surprise.

'Yes,' I said, 'I am, but why do you ask?'

'Because, Agha, they say that most *feringhis* are, and up there is a *naqsh*, a carving, which is very old.'

I had read of ancient rock carvings at Sar-i-Pul, believed to be Akkadian. I hesitated. The afternoon was wearing on. It meant explanations to the escort and I remembered the customs official's warning. I decided to push on.

There was little to see, anyway, Abdul said, and tomorrow there would be more.

I asked him how he had learned about such things, and he said his father had taught him. His father had been *mirza* (secretary) to the Deputy Governor of Shiraz.

I said I thought his home was Isfahan. He explained that it was later, but that he had been born in Shiraz. His father was very well educated and had taught him to read and write when still an infant, and he added that, of course, the language of Shiraz was the purest Persian in the whole country. He told me also that his father had many enemies, who by intrigue caused him to be dismissed and transferred to Isfahan.

Abdul paused as I slowed down to avoid a drove of donkeys, heavily laden with pieces of rock.

'For roadmaking,' Abdul glanced round at them. 'Fifteen donkey-loads, but the contractor will assuredly charge the Government for thirty loads.' He spat contemptuously.

The road continued to climb with long steep gradients, twisting like a gigantic snake as it rounded the winding contours of the treeless boulder-strewn spurs of the Zagros mountains.

For a considerable distance Zobeida ground her way slowly upwards in low gear, and for the last several kilometres the water in the radiator boiled furiously. At last we reached the top, the famous Paitak Pass, gateway to the great plateau. We had climbed 8,000 feet from the level of the plain and, all being well, I reckoned we should reach Kermanshah just before dusk.

The air was quite chilly up in the pass, but the radiator cap was too hot to touch. With a piece of cloth I carefully unscrewed it and jumped quickly back as a jet of steam and boiling water spouted up. I had forgotten the effect of altitude on steam pressure and was lucky to escape a scalding. I filled the radiator with fresh water and waited a few minutes to allow the engine to cool while I observed the scenery, and the escort got out and stretched their legs.

We were now in the homeland of the Iranian Kurds and again I remembered the warning of the official at the frontier post to be sure to reach the town of Kermanshah before nightfall. The afternoon was already well advanced, but the stiffest climbs were now behind us. We would be running downhill most of the way to Karind, and beyond that the road should present no particular problem.

There was less motor traffic than I had expected for a main highway. This was fortunate considering the bad state of the road and the frequent hairpin bends. It was difficult enough dealing with the many mules and donkeys and occasional strings of camels. Usually we seemed to come upon these round some blind corner, and I would have to jam on the brakes to avoid running into them. On these occasions Abdul would fire off some pungent good-natured invective at the muleteers, to which they would reply in kind without even looking up, as they whacked and dragged their beasts to the side of the roadway.

'You seem to know how to talk to these people like one of them,' I said.

'*Beli*, Agha,' he laughed, 'why not, because I *am* one of them.'

'*Chirra*, Abdul, you a *charvadar*, a driver of mules?'

'Never, Agha, but I have lived on the road and know these people well.'

'Tell me about how you lived on the road.'

He was silent for a few moments and threw a quick glance at me. 'I only fear you may laugh at me,' he said.

'A humorous story's better than a sad one,' I replied, 'and laughter is better than weeping.'

'True, Agha, then I will tell you. The happening was of this manner. When my parents died and I was left alone, I was still very young. One day, I was sitting on the steps of the mosque of Lutfullah in Isfahan, when a stranger came up and spoke to me. He was of ripe years, and his beard was dyed red. He wore the green turban of a Saiyid, and he told me his name was Meshedi Abbas. He said he had known my father and explained that he himself was the warden of a wayside shrine on this very road we are following now.'

At this point I slowed down to pass a man riding on a donkey and leading a string of three mules. They were carrying bulging panniers and were taking up most of the road. The second mule had a young goat tied to its back, and the third one had several scrawny fowl tethered by the legs to the panniers. The man was sitting as usual at the tail-end of the donkey and swinging his legs to the rhythm of the animal's steps. Abdul exchanged a *Salaam aleikum* with him as we passed, and then continued with the story.

'The old Saiyid asked me many questions about myself, and seemed to take a fancy to me. He said he was getting old and needed somebody of my age and intelligence to help him with the shrine, and to make agreeable conversation with passing travellers so that they would stop and rest awhile.'

Abdul nearly slipped off his seat as I swerved quickly to avoid a deep cavity in the road, and then continued.

'The Saiyid promised me a small percentage of the takings and said these would depend on how cleverly I talked to people. As I saw no other means of livelihood in Isfahan I agreed, and two or three days later I went with him and together we came down the road.'

'This same road we are on now?'

'*Beli*, Agha, this very same road. In a few minutes I will show you the place where our shrine was. I was disappointed when I first saw it. I had expected something more imposing, but the tomb itself was well kept, and by gradually adding extra stones I was able to improve it. This pleased the old man, whose back was bent with age, and he was content to sit smoking his hookah and leave me to carry the water-jars and see that the water-pipes were kept filled ready for any passers-by.'

'And did many of them stop?'

'*Beli*, Agha. The road is long and tiring, as your Honour can see, and few failed to step aside and enjoy a drink of fresh water and a pull at the hookah. And in their gratitude some would leave a small coin and invoke a blessing.'

'Wayfarers are usually generous,' I said.

He shrugged. 'Some are, but many are not. Yet in a good season we would do well, for our expenses were little. I only received a small share of the takings, but I could see that to be custodian of a shrine was a profitable business. Your Honour would be surprised at the amount of money we made.'

'Why then did you give it up?' I asked.

'To tell you the truth, Agha, I had no complaint about either the business or my old master, even though he did pay me so very little, but I became weary of the solitude. I very seldom saw any young people, and I began to long for the life of the city and the excitement of the bazaars. So I decided to quit my master and go to Qazvin. I had saved sufficient money to buy a donkey from a passing caravan. It was an old beast and in bad condition, but I paid very little for it and it would carry me as far as Qazvin. After that I would not need it.'

There was another pause as we rounded a sharp bend. I jammed on the brakes and barely missed three men walking down the middle of the road. They were wild-looking characters, and carried rifles.

'Kurds,' said Abdul in an undertone, and quickly shouted '*Salaam aleikum*!' The men gave a rather surly reply, and scowled as we passed.

'Are they road-guards or tribesmen?' I asked Abdul.

'*Che arz kunam*. Guards or tribesmen, all are thieves in this part of the country, but,' after a quick glance behind, 'Allah be praised! they have gone on.'

'*Alhamud-ul-illah*,' echoed the escort, gripping their rifles. 'They were Kurds, but they have gone their way in peace.'

'Continue your story,' I said. 'What did your master say when you left him?'

'My master was sorry to lose me. He made me promise to stay till the end of the pilgrimage season and then I took leave of him. He wished me *Khuda hafiz*, god-speed, and I started off up the road on my donkey. The weather was very hot. There had been no rain, and the crops and grass were parched. Also the previous harvest had been a bad one so that there was almost a famine. The hillsides were scorched brown and there was no grazing.

'By the time I got to Hamadan my ass was so weak, he could hardly walk. His ears hung down like an old hag's breasts and his knees knocked with every step. I pushed on and made two more short marches, resting the animal every *farsakh*. Finally he could go no farther. He lay down and there by the roadside he died.'

Abdul was enjoying his narration. He paused dramatically and awaited my comment. I murmured something about ill fortune, and he continued: 'Your Honour speaks truly, and I cursed myself for having been cheated by those sons of burnt fathers who had sold me an animal that was already half dead. Then as I sat down to rest awhile, and watched the flies settling round the dead beast's eyes, I had a beautiful idea. That miserable *oolagh* had cost me good money, earned with the sweat of my body. Now, dead as he was, he should earn it back for me. My pride was injured for having been made a fool of. My face blackened and I swore I would not show myself in the city until I had made good the loss.' Again he paused for effect and I grunted to show I was listening.

'So I set to work and scraped a hole in the ground by the roadside, under the mulberry tree beneath which I had taken shelter from the sun. By Allah, the earth was hard, but I finally had the hole big enough and then I dragged the donkey into it and covered him up with earth and stones. I was very tired, but I rested a little and then I collected some larger rocks and constructed a tomb over the mound. At a little distance I found a small spring of water. I filled the jar I had brought with me and placed it by the tomb. Then I stretched my rug under the tree and sat there and prayed to Allah.'

Again Abdul paused. The picture was so comical, I laughed aloud and the two *tufangchis* joined in.

'Caravans and mule trains passed and though few of them stopped, some of them threw me a coin. Each evening after prayer-time I added just one or two more rocks, carefully and very gradually building up the tomb. And the caravan folk and others would see me sitting there in silent contemplation. Some would greet me; others would wonder and exclaim "*Wah! Wah! Afireen!*" Why had they not noticed this *ziaret* (shrine) before? And if one of them flung a coin, muttering Allah is Great, others would do the same. And it was so successful that I tarried there, for this was more profitable than anything I could hope to find in Qazvin, and I did not have to share my earnings with anyone else.'

'Wah! Wah!' murmured the escort approvingly in the back of the car.

'The months passed: the donkey had long since been paid for, and in addition the shrine was becoming more beautiful every day. By this time it really looked like a *ziaret* and not a mere roadside grave. Also people who passed frequently had become accustomed to it. They never noticed the gradual additions, and accepted it as always having been there. Some few who did notice its growth shook their heads and muttered, "Allah is indeed Great! This shrine must be that of a powerful saint, for it grows by miracles." And their donations increased as befitted a wonder-working shrine.'

'Is this mound—tomb—still there?' I asked

'Surely it is there, Agha, for who could remove it? When we come to the place, I will show you.'

I supposed this to be the end of the story, but Abdul had not yet finished. There was evidently a sequel, and he continued: 'Well one day, to my great surprise, who should come along up the road, but my old master himself. He had grown much older, but we recognised each other at once. He threw his arms around me and we embraced. He stayed awhile and he told me that misfortune had overtaken him. There had been a great storm somewhere up in the mountains, and the stream had suddenly poured down in a great torrent. In its force it had washed away a great portion of the bank, and the entire *ziaret* had been swept away with it.

'"Wah! Wah!" I said with real compassion. "Truly the ways of Allah are past understanding.

'"W'Allah!" he replied, "but so it was written. My day had come." He was silent for a few moments, and I saw him looking thoughtfully at the tomb. Then he came out with it. "Tell me, my son," he asked, "how did you manage to become warden of such an important shrine? I do not recall seeing this when last I came down this road many summers ago. Who is the saint who lies in this very fine tomb?"

'I was at a loss to know what to say, and tried to talk of something else. But when he saw me hesitate, he pressed me all the more, and, being taken by surprise, I had to confess the truth.'

'"Your donkey! My son," he said, "joke not with an old man!"

'"*Nakhair, Agha*," I said, "by my eyes, it is the truth," and I told him the story. And then a thought came suddenly to me. "Agha," I said, "All the time I served you, I never once asked you the name of the saint in your *ziaret*."

'"My son," said the old man, "my years weigh heavily upon me. The *ziaret* has been destroyed anyway and it is no longer of any importance, but since you ask I will be equally truthful with you." He looked up and down the road as though afraid someone might hear him. Then he leaned towards me and whispered in my ear "My son, *shuturem bud* . . . It was my camel."'

There was silence for a moment. Abdul looked at me and we both laughed, and the *tufangchis* joined in. It was a good story, well told, and I complimented him. 'Truly, Abdul, your real occupation should be that of Teller of Tales.'

'*Che arz kunam*, Agha,' he shrugged. 'Many are the tales I could tell you; some of them true, some not, but often the true ones are the more *ajeeb* and unbelievable.'

About half an hour later, the road crossed a culvert spanning a stream-bed full of boulders. The stream was almost dry, but its channel ran steeply between two spurs of the higher range, and in the rainy season it would no doubt become a raging torrent.

Abdul pointed with his finger as we reached the culvert.

'Look Agha, see that big rock at the edge of the nullah? That's just about where the old Saiyid's *ziaret* . . . used to be.' His voice dropped, and he seemed taken aback. 'W'Allah, but that rock was not there in my time, and the stream-bed is much changed.' We drove on in silence for a few minutes. 'But, *insh'allah*, Agha, you will see that my *ziaret* will still be standing, because there was no stream to wash it away.'

Viewed from a distance Kermanshah looked reasonably impressive. In the oblique rays of the late afternoon sun its walls and buildings appeared a solid mass of golden masonry against the green of the surrounding vegetation. But as we approached, the effect of light and colour faded, and grey mud walls dispelled the illusion of masonry. By the time we reached the outskirts, Kermanshah appeared just as drab, dirty and uninspiring as the great majority of towns in this part of the world.

I halted at what might be described as a combined inn and coaching station. It was dimly lit by a few flickering electric lamps, and somewhere in the vicinity was the noisily chugging gas-engine which generated the current.

The two *tufangchis* unscrambled themselves from the pile of baggage and, looking more than ever like bandits in the failing light, they came forward and thanked me for the ride. Then they faded into the shadows.

Next moment I was greeted by an important-looking individual with a metal badge on his inverted pudding-bowl of a hat. He was the bank *ghulam*, waiting to guide me to the manager's house.

Before leaving London I had lunched with a top executive of the Imperial Bank of Persia at his club. Afterwards, we had sat over coffee near a large window overlooking Pall Mall and continued to discuss my forthcoming journey. I had asked for some final tips of the road.

'You know the language and you're no stranger to the East,' the director said, 'but there's one piece of advice I can give you. Never, never sleep in an Iranian caravanserai or local inn. In a big town, the bank manager or the consul will always be glad to put you up. We've written to all our branch managers, informing them of your journey. We have a branch in every sizeable town as you know, and you should make a point of calling on them at once, advising them in advance when possible—but never, never stay in a caravanserai. They're filthy and full of typhus germs. If you cannot reach a town with a bank manager, then sleep out in the open, no matter what the weather.'

I did not tell him that I had slept in caravanserais in eastern Iran and had resolved never to do so again, but promised to take his advice, and I had written to the Kermanshah manager from Baghdad, informing him of my journey and expected date of arrival.

Now the bank *ghulam* assumed charge of everything. The manager gave me a warm welcome, including the much appreciated luxury of a hot bath before dinner.

Chapter 6

HAMADAN

Since Kermanshah the road had had many ups and downs, but for the last part of the journey it climbed steadily until we reached Hamadan, which lies at a height of 6,280 feet above sea-level on the northern slope of Mount Elvend, whose summit towers up nearly as high again. In contrast with much of the lower-lying country we had passed through, where spring had already arrived, here the landscape was bare and windswept and snow lay deep on the nearby mountain slopes.

My first view of the town was disappointingly grey and colourless. I had expected something rather more impressive from a city that had been the capital of a succession of imperial dynasties. I could not even see any outstanding ruins, only a conglomeration of bare mud-coloured walls and featureless buildings, with a foreground of broken wasteland formed by the debris of centuries.

However, the bleakness of the scene was quickly compensated for by the warm hospitality of the bank manager. From him I obtained all the information I desired about local conditions. I spent the whole of the next day chatting with the city's leading merchants and notables, but they were not able to add much to what I had already learned from my host.

I found them friendly, but parochial in their interests and generally ill-informed on anything beyond their own immediate boundaries. This was not surprising when one considered that even the smallest Iranian towns are to a great extent self-sufficient in their daily needs. Each bazaar is a small-scale replica of the larger markets. Each possesses its own sources of local produce, its native crafts and industry, its metal-workers, tanners, shoemakers, dyers, spinners and weavers, millers, butchers, bakers and the rest of them. This limits their need for contact with the outside world and, lacking such contact, they are thrown back upon their own society, and are slow to open up to a stranger, particularly to a *feringhi*.

In their domestic life, Iranians are lovers of privacy and they seek to ensure this by enclosing themselves within high walls. From the outside, these walls are dull, ugly, and uninspiring, and to the stranger in the street what goes on behind them is cloaked in mystery.

The big wooden entrance door is kept locked, but one may just happen along as the bars and bolts are withdrawn to allow a black-draped figure to slip through, accompanied if she is young by an older, stouter, similarly draped person. The two then glide, rather than walk, along the dusty alleyway to the bazaars.

In the fleeting moment before the door has time to close, the passer-by may glimpse a flash of colour, the red of roses or the turquoise blue or viridian green of tilework, but for the rest his curiosity must content itself with the sprays of peach or pomegranate peeping tantalisingly over the crest of the wall.

But walls do not convey the same appearance of age as does masonry. Stonework weathers and develops a mellow beauty of its own, but sun-dried brick, as distinct from the kiln-dried product, slowly disintegrates into the earth from which it originated. Old walls may be patched up and mud-plastered anew, which makes it difficult to distinguish ancient from modern, while their appearance remains monotonous.

Hamadan's long history is proven by authentic records. The Greeks called it Ekbatana, and it was probably ancient before the Medes made it their seat of government. Then, when Cyrus revolted in 553 BC and founded the Achaemenian dynasty, he made Ekbatana his summer capital.

In the Old Testament Ekbatana is referred to as Achmetha, and we are told that during the first year of the reign of Cyrus the King had decreed that the temple in Jerusalem should be rebuilt. However, the work was held up by conflicting influences, and it was not until Darius I had succeeded to the throne in 521 BC that a search was made in the royal archives and 'there was found at Achmeta in the palace . . . a roll, and therein was a record thus written: In the first year of Cyrus the King the same Cyrus, made a decree concerning the house of God at Jerusalem, Let the house be builded.' (Ezra VI, 1–3)

I had read somewhere, I believe it was Polybius, a reference to the fine buildings of Ekbatana, and I had hoped that some remains of these might still be visible. But it was Baghdad all over again. There had been too much destruction. This time it had not been the Mongols (they had come upon the scene many centuries later), but Alexander the Great who had done the most thorough wrecking, and had stripped off all the gold panelling and silver tilework from the royal palace. What little that was not carried away by the Macedonians was looted during the succeeding reign of the Seleucid monarchs.

The first ancient monument I visited was the alleged tomb of Esther and Mordecai. According to the Old Testament (Esther II, 8–9), Esther, a Jewish girl of great beauty, became the favourite queen of King Ahasuerus, who 'reigned from India even unto Ethiopia' and whose royal capital was Shushan (Susa). King Ahasuerus is today widely accepted as being identical with Xerxes I, who succeeded his father, the Achaemenian Darius I in 485 BC and probably used Ekbatana as his summer seat.

Esther's uncle Mordecai was the victim of anti-Jewish intrigue, but through his niece's intervention he found grace with the King and eventually became the most powerful man in the realm, second only to the monarch himself.

Part of the legend associating Esther with Ekbatana credits the Queen with having established the first Jewish colony in that city. But while it is certain that a Jewish community was founded there at an early date, there is no known record of any direct connection between Esther or Mordecai and Ekbatana, or of their having been buried there.

Professor Herzfeld, in his *Archaeological History of Iran* (p. 106) points out that the Jewish colony in Ekbatana was actually founded by Queen Shushadukht (Susanna), the wife of the Sasanian King Yezdegird I, early in the fourth century AD and that it is this lady whose remains lie in the Hamadan tomb, while those of Esther would have been laid to rest in Susa fully eight centuries earlier.

The tomb is solidly built with thick plastered walls and surmounted by a plain brickwork dome. It is venerated by both Jews and Moslems, the latter regarding it as the shrine of some early holy man. The structure is unquestionably ancient, but I would have said the architecture was Arab and dated at the earliest from the eighth or ninth century AD.

With Abdul's story of those other 'tombs' fresh in my mind, I felt sceptical about all ancient shrines and their reputed occupants. Did the tomb of Zobeida in Baghdad, I wondered, really contain the remains of Harun-ar-Rashid's favourite wife? Allah alone knows.

But Queen Susanna was mainly famous for another reason. She was the mother of King Bahram Gur, the 'Great Hunter' whose exploits in the chase form the basis for many popular Persian legends. The country around Ekbatana abounded in game of all kinds, big and small, including lion and the wild ass, which were the King's favourite quarry. He prided himself on his skill with the bow, and the story goes that on one occasion, when he was accompanied by a favourite handmaiden, his shooting was not up to his usual standard. After some particularly bad misses the girl rashly made some derogatory remark about his marksmanship which so outraged the King that he aimed an arrow at her, and this time hit the mark.

Ekbatana retained its importance throughout the Sasanian period until the disastrous defeat of the Iranian army at Nihavand in AD 644, after which its status was reduced to that of a minor provincial capital. It was the home of the great scientist and philosopher, Ali-al-Hussein ibn Sina, better known in the West as Avicena, who lived AD 980–1036, and is buried in Hamadan. His tomb, fully authenticated, still survives and was restored as recently as 1877. Hamadan's fortunes improved when, in the late eleventh century, the Seljuq Sultans moved their seat there from Baghdad, and it remained their capital for the next fifty years. The Seljuqs greatly embellished the city, and one of their finest buildings, the Gunbad-i-Alaviyan, was constructed as a mausoleum for the influential Alavi family. The Gunbad (the word means mausoleum) is still standing, and while the building itself is very dilapidated, much of the splendid stucco scroll-work in the interior has miraculously survived the vicissitudes of eight hundred years and two Mongol invasions.

One thing the ruins of ancient Ekbatana have in common with those of Babylon is the statue of a lion. There it lay, time-weathered and mutilated, on the outskirts of the town. The statue is the sole remaining vestige in Hamadan of the Parthian epoch (248 BC–AD 224). The story goes that the lion, possibly one of a pair, originally stood at the main gate of the city, and that early in the tenth century the Dailamite tribesmen attacked and captured Hamadan. Their leader took a fancy to the old Parthian lion and wanted to carry it off as a trophy. But the statue was too heavy and after suffering some damage it was abandoned outside the town.

Abdul, of course, had his own version. He maintained that the lion commemorated the hunting prowess of his favourite hero, Rustam. Hamadan, he said, had produced fine men in those days, but today the Hamadanis were *wahshi* (barbarians).

He was not impressed by Hamadan. 'Wait until you see Isfahan and Shiraz,' he told me, and quoted an old pun. '*Ham-dani hich na-dani*,' meaning 'Know-all knows nothing.'

And as we picked our way through the mounds and rubble of what, until the Mongols came, had been streets and dwellings, he appeared disgruntled and ill at ease. '*Che faida darad*?' he grumbled. 'What's the use of walking through all this debris and *biaban*? This place is full of evil spirits. Better let them rest in peace lest evil befall us.'

Chapter 7

QAZVIN—TABRIZ

From Hamadan onwards the landscape continued dismal and windswept, and the general drabness was relieved only by glimpses of distant snow-covered mountains and occasional coffee-coloured villages. These were saved from utter dreariness by their encircling belt of emerald-green vegetation—alfalfa, barley, or other fodder-crops—with a few slender poplars, a willow or a mulberry tree or two, marking the course of an irrigation channel.

Every few kilometres we passed a *chae-khaneh*, a wayside tea-house. In Iran, the *chae-khaneh* is as much a national institution as are public houses in Britain, and just as welcome a sight to the weary traveller on a long journey. However remote the *chae-khaneh* from the nearest village, there would usually be at least a mule or donkey tethered or hobbled outside, while its master sat within, sipping his glass of tea, or sucking in lungfuls of pungent smoke from a *qalian*.

If the landscape lacked life and interest, we found plenty on the road itself. We passed large numbers of *fourgons*, a type of four-wheeled covered wagon, resembling the 'prairie-schooners' of the American Wild West, but drawn by four horses abreast. These *fourgons* are Russian in origin, and the Russians are said to have adopted both the pattern of vehicle and the name from Napoleon's armies, who used them as military transport.

To me these *fourgons* were the most picturesque of all the road traffic we encountered. Their horses were usually well matched both as to size and colour, and appeared to be all in good condition. The driver, swathed in a heavy sheepskin kaftan, lay rolled up on, and sometimes inside, a Persian carpet, and as often as not was asleep.

The horses had bells on their harness and kept up a merry jingling, which probably had a soporific effect upon the driver. I noticed that the leading *fourgon*—there are nearly always a train of them—carried some special mascot in the form of a branch of pine tree, a bunch of flowers, a brass ornament or other trifle, fastened to the front of the roof. The wagons were mostly heavily laden and appeared to be carrying merchandise imported from Russia—largely cotton piece-goods, sugar and kerosene.

The drivers were nearly all Azerbaijan Tatars. They were grim as well as grimy-looking creatures, who unlike the cheerful Iranian *charvadars* rarely responded to a greeting, or did so with a scowl. We passed hundreds of these *fourgons*, and I wondered how one would fare if one came across them on some narrow mountain road. Later, I would learn the answer to that question in what was to be one of the narrowest escapes of my life.

Alternating with the wagon trains were numerous camel caravans, headed always by a man riding a donkey. Abdul assured me that unless they were led by the donkey the camels refused to march.

I remember when I was living in Constantinople on the Grande Rue de Pera, I heard a great hubbub in the street one day, and saw an extraordinary sight. A long string of camels were marching with their usual sedate gait down the Grande Rue, preceded, of course, by the donkey and its rider. Something frightened the donkey and he shied, kicked his heels in the air, and threw his master. Then he bolted along the street, braying loudly, with the whole camel train careering after him, shedding their burdens and scattering the traffic right and left.

Some of the southbound caravans we met were laden with Russian benzine or kerosene packed in big sheet-iron drums, each containing some forty pounds of weight of fuel. These had all been shipped across the Caspian from the Baku refineries.

We overtook numerous strings of pack mules, jingling with bells and fully laden with merchandise, including chests of tea from India and bales of cotton piece-goods from Britain. All this had been carried by sea to Basreh, thence by river upstream to Baghdad, and finally by pack animal along this ancient trade route on its way to Tehran and distant points beyond.

There is something soothing about the deliberate, measured gait of a caravan of camels. With their humps and heavy burdens swaying in concerted rhythm and their long, loosely jointed limbs swinging in regular, unvarying tempo, the flat, padded feet tread the ground with a shuffling springy step, as though reluctant to disturb the dust of ages.

The camel has his own standard of time and distance. The one constant factor about him is his rate of march. The baggage-camel travels at a steady two and a half miles per hour, and thereby sets the pace for the entire convoy. The unknown factors of his progress include such elements as flash floods and spates, which may wash away a stretch of road or make it dangerously slippery, landslides, which may block the trail, or snow, which may close the passes. His marches are measured neither by milestones nor by hours, but by water-holes and camping grounds.

Even though his nose be linked to his brother's tail, the camel never relaxes his attitude of dignified superiority and looks down with supercilious contempt upon more rapid forms of transportation and their human perpetrators.

There is no doubt that he considers himself the Brahmin of the animal world. And Arab Beduin, born and bred in the same camp with their camels, recognise this feeling of superiority and treat it with respect. For is it not a fact, they say, that of the one hundred sacred names of Allah, only ninety-nine are known to the human race, but that the Prophet (on whom be peace!) whispered the hundredth name to the camel, which explains that animal's self-righteous expression as he looks down with half-closed eyes upon his two-legged inferiors.

Within an hour after leaving Hamadan we came to a very bad stretch of roadway. Winter snow and spring rains had worked havoc with the surface, and its condition was so atrocious that higher authority had evidently decreed that something must be done about it.

This was one of the very few places on the whole journey where we came upon any sign of recent road repairs. At this point Abdul nudged my arm and remarked: 'A little way farther up on the right, Agha, is the place I told you about where I built my *ziaret*.'

At that moment I was so occupied in steering the car between half-filled pot-holes and patches of broken rock, that I did not immediately grasp what he meant. Then I remembered.

'You mean where you buried your donkey?'

'*Beli*, Agha.' He pointed ahead. 'It is close to that mulberry tree, just by the roadside yonder.'

I was still too busy picking my way to pay attention to any mulberry tree, but a few moments later Abdul uttered what sounded like a groan of despair.

'*Piderha-sukhte*! Sons of burnt fathers!'

'What's the matter, Abdul?' I asked, as I swerved to avoid a gaping hole.

'The matter, Agha? Look!' He pointed with his finger. 'There, under that tree. That's where my *ziaret* stood, right there.'

'I don't see any shrine,' I said, stopping the car.

'No, Agha, there is nothing there. Nothing at all.' His voice was bitter with disappointment, then hardened with anger. 'Those lazy sons of burnt fathers have stolen all the rocks and stones—all *my* rocks and stones that I collected—stolen them to mend the road! May they burn with their unmentionable fathers! Allah wither their roots and blight their offspring!'

For the most of the way since leaving Hamadan we had been driving into a bitter head-wind. Blowing fresh from the Central Asian steppes, it lashed our faces and hands with the sharp sting of a cossack knout. It sent dust-devils dancing and spiralling along the road, and it peppered the windscreen with grit and gravel.

As the afternoon advanced, the sky became grey and

overcast and there was a hint of snow in the air. We had only another ten kilometres left to Qazvin, but there was no Imperial bank in that town, though I understood there was a reasonably good hotel and I wanted to get there before dark so as to be sure of getting a room.

We came to a wayside *chae-khaneh*, and since both Abdul and I were chilled to the bone, and there was no need for hurry, I pulled up the car and we went inside. There were several ponies and donkeys tethered outside, and as we entered the low-roofed structure, and came from daylight into the thick smoke-laden atmosphere, the place seemed to be crowded with people. The air was heavy with tobacco smoke mingled with the acrid fumes from both a glowing charcoal brazier and a massive brass samovar, and it was further enriched with the odour of unwashed human bodies and sweaty travel-stained clothing.

For a few minutes my eyes smarted and watered and my lungs nearly choked with the fumes and smoke. Then gradually I began to discern figures seated on low stools at rough wooden benches or tables. These were the owners of the animals outside, and the steady murmur of their voices as they exchanged the gossip of the road was punctuated by the bubbling of the water in the *qalian* bowls.

Viewed in the murky half-light, the effect was almost eerie, as one muffled figure after another would reach over, grasp the stem of the *qalian*, raise the mouthpiece to his lips and inhale deeply. He would fill his lungs to coughing point with the pungent fumes and then exhale slowly and deliberately a jet of bluish-grey smoke.

Abdul and I seated ourselves on a couple of spare stools, and ordered a glass of tea each.

'*Bi-chashm*! By my eyes!' The *ghulam*, or servant of the tea-house, took my order. Through the thick haze I could discern the dull yellow glint of the tarnished brass samovar, heroic in its dimensions and kept permanently on the boil to provide hot water for the tea.

I watched the *ghulam* produce a couple of small tea-glasses, and hoped they had been washed after the last user. He poured into each a little tea from a diminutive chinaware pot, and then filled them up with boiling water from the samovar. Sugar was added, and the resulting beverage was hot, sweet and refreshing. I sipped it with a sense of satisfaction, tempered by the thought that the water, before going into the samovar, had been collected in a kerosene tin from the *joob* (water channel) outside. It was mere chance that, as we came out from the stifling atmosphere of the tea-house, and I murmured something to Abdul about the refreshing effects of a glass of hot tea, my eyes fell on the *joob*. There, floating in the very middle of it, was a dead cat.

It was early evening by the time we reached Qazvin, and as at Hamadan my first impression was one of disappointment. From its position on the map I had expected something more exciting, for here is the meeting place of four main highways—to Tehran and Khorasan, to Resht and the Caspian, to Tabriz and the Caucasus, and the road we had just travelled on, to Hamadan and eventually Baghdad.

In such a key position I had visions of extensive bazaars and caravanserais, with modern conveniences for the traveller to the extent of at least one presentable hotel. In the event I found nothing of the sort.

But few towns are seen at their best when one arrives tired and numbed after driving for hours in an open car against a bitter head-wind. Besides which, the daylight was already fading and visibility was not improved by the thick dust-laden atmosphere, blended with the smoke from scores of cooking-fires.

We entered the town through an arched gateway decorated with shiny ceramic tilework in which bright yellow and green with some blue were the salient colours. The archway had little architectural merit and in the greyness of the gathering dusk its gay colouring merely gave it a tawdry appearance.

We bumped our way down a long dusty thoroughfare lined with trees, then turned into a narrow side-street. We inched through a teeming medley of camels, horses, donkeys and pedestrians, sounding our horn continuously, but fruitlessly, since its warning sound went unnoticed in the general clamour. Once I had to stop dead while a big fat-tailed sheep was dragged bodily from between Zobeida's front wheels. The road was lined with tea-houses and entrances to serais, evoking memories of the Nimak Mandi bazaar in Peshawar City.

The smells were also very similar, and now, being the hour for the evening meal, the predominant odour was an appetising blend of wood and charcoal smoke, cooking fat, and roasting *kebabs*. The very thought of *kebabs* sharpened the growing pangs of hunger, and I looked forward with keen anticipation to a hot meal. But first I must find a room for the night.

We came upon the hotel round the next corner. It had been described to me as reasonably good, but it turned out to be a shabby hostelry and in no sense a modern hotel. Adjoining it was a large open courtyard or serai, and as I drove into this I saw that it already contained a varied collection of transport, ancient and modern. There were several big American cars, including a couple of early-model Cadillacs and a more recent Dodge. All were dirty and looked much the worse for wear. Of their drivers and passengers there was no sign. I supposed they were either in the hotel or in the nearby restaurant. The cars were all piled high with baggage and merchandise. Bales, bundles, tin trunks and bulging saddle-bags were slung and roped over the roof, sides and bumpers of each car. On the roof of the Dodge, a she-goat and a bundle of bedraggled hens were trussed with cords.

Apart from the cars a number of horses and ponies, tethered with heel-ropes, were nosing hungrily into a heap of *jau*, or green barley, that had been flung down in front of them. There were also numerous donkeys, secured with one fore and one hind leg tightly hobbled together.

My hopes of finding accommodation fell when I saw all these signs of travellers, and my fears were confirmed when I called at the office for a room. 'Very sorry, but the hotel is full,' I was told, 'but perhaps, if you don't mind sharing a room?'

This was a disappointment and I did some quick thinking. I had wanted to see something of Qazvin. Despite my initial impression, it must have a fair-sized trading community. Perhaps it would be better to stay one night only, and push on the next day to Tabriz. I would have to come back to Qazvin anyway. I said I would look at the room, and the clerk handed me a key.

The room was bad, but it might have been worse. There was one wooden bedstead and one of iron. Fortunately the other party had already taken the wooden one, a well-roped saddle-bag marked his prior possession.

Just as well, I thought; the miserable iron camp-bed would be more uncomfortable but less insanitary and less lively. In any case I had my own bedding, but before carrying it all up I was curious to get a glimpse of my room-mate. In all circumstances, I could not very well pick and choose my sleeping companions, but I could at least be careful. I left everything in the car with Abdul in charge and went off to a neighbouring eating-house.

Inside, the air was thick, but the place was not too crowded. After disposing of a piled plate of rice and *kebab*, washed down with a couple of glasses of hot tea, I felt much refreshed. I returned to the hotel and revisited the bedroom and this time I found the other party in possession.

He was the biggest and most picturesque specimen of a Kurd I had ever seen outside of a picture-book. His size was enhanced by the lofty native head-dress. I expected to find him armed to the teeth, but his only visible weapon was a silver-hilted *khanjar*, or dagger, which protruded from the multifolds of his waistband.

More impressive than the dagger, however, was a large *qalian*, or water-pipe. It was a fine specimen of noble proportions, and would not have been unworthy of the Shah himself. It had an intricately carved silver top-piece to hold the tobacco and a very elaborately decorated water bowl. The mouthpiece was probably amber. It marked the owner as a person of importance, a tribal chieftain, perhaps.

The Kurd was squatting comfortably on his bed with the

qalian propped up beside him, which is how I had such a clear view of it. He was inhaling great mouthfuls of smoke, drawing it deep down into his lungs, and then exhaling it in long blue streamers which curled up towards the solitary electric light bulb hanging from the ceiling. The bulb was dirty and fly-blown and gave out a pallid flickering light that threatened to fail at any moment.

The Kurd's face wore a vague far-away expression, as though he were dreaming of some Kurdish Scheherazade. His eyelids did not move, nor did his expression change, but his lips framed the words *Salaam aleikum.* I nodded politely, returned his greeting and withdrew. The air in the room was almost unbreathable.

I went back to the serai and sent Abdul off to get his own meal. Meanwhile, I remained sitting in the car, thinking things over. I felt this was getting me nowhere. I had been driving all day and would be driving again early next morning. I needed sleep. Abdul returned within the half-hour and I decided to have one more look at the room. By this time the Kurd might have gone to sleep and the atmosphere might have cleared.

I went silently upstairs. The door of the room was shut, but I could hear voices inside. I hesitated a moment, then quietly opened the door a mere crack. Through the thick pungent smoke and by the pale flickering light I could see that there were now two Kurds. My original room-mate was still squatting on his bed and his companion had drawn up the iron bedstead close to the other and was sitting on it, with the *qalian* between them. They were so engrossed in their conversation that they did not notice the door open. Nor, probably, did they observe it close quietly behind me.

Apart from anything else, those pungent fumes settled the question. For a moment, their peculiar acrid tang puzzled me, then I placed it. They had mixed strong raw opium with their tobacco. A powerful mixture.

With a little trouble I rearranged the baggage in the car and was able to stretch out my legs and sleep fitfully, but in reasonable comfort. At least the air was fresh.

Abdul, enveloped in his sheepskin kaftan, with his old rug rolled around him, had found a comfortable resting place in a heap of chopped straw. He slept much more soundly than I did, for I was awakened repeatedly by the braying of donkeys tethered within a few metres of me. Then, with at least another hour to daybreak, the neighbouring bazaar began to come to life. With my legs stiff and numb from the cold, I struggled out of the car, woke up Abdul and we went along to the nearby tea-house, where we found the samovar already simmering and the air warm with thick tobacco smoke. After a glass of hot tea and about one square yard of newly baked *churek*, my blood began to circulate, and I felt ready for the road.

Churek is a common form of native bread. It comes freshly made in a moist, under-baked condition, in limp, flannel-like slabs or sheets, slightly smaller than a newspaper, and has the consistency and roughly the flavour of an Indian *chupatti*. It looks very indigestible, but tastes good when dry. My way of dealing with it on the journey was unorthodox but effective. I spread the huge slabs over my chest as I drove, and in a very short time they dried and became as crisp and brittle as biscuit. Once dry, the bread will keep fresh for days, and on the road I fared very well and kept very fit on a simple diet of hard-boiled eggs, hot sugared tea without milk, and sun-dried *churek*.

The day broke cloudy and a cold breeze was blowing up the dust, straw and other litter in the open courtyard of the serai. It was not a morning for sightseeing or bazaar visiting. In any case we would be back again fairly soon from Tabriz. *Insh'allah*, by then the weather might be less unpleasant.

For the first time Zobeida gave trouble in starting. Clearly she also disliked the cold and it was only after repeated bouts with the starting handle that we got the engine to fire, and were able to move off.

From Qazvin to Tabriz, as the crow flies, is a little over 400 kilometres, but extra allowance must be made for stretches of winding road in the hilly regions and in traversing one particularly difficult mountain range which we would encounter further north.

The first portion of the road after leaving Qazvin led through an area of agricultural land. A little later, in the spring, the countryside would be aglow with peach, apricot and other fruit blossom, but now it was bare, with little vegetation to relieve the general drabness, though an unmistakable sign of its agricultural character were the numerous *joobs* which we encountered.

In Iran, a *joob* is water-channel. It may be a mere shallow depression or a deep ditch; it may be a narrow drain, a few inches in width, or it may be several feet across. Whatever the size, *joobs* since time immemorial have played an important role in Iranian daily life, in every centre of habitation as well as in the open country. They run along the main streets of the bigger cities, and flow through the principal thoroughfare and perhaps a few alleyways of the smaller towns. Every village has its *joob*, and so has nearly every tea-house. One comes across them in the most unlikely places, and sometimes far from any visible habitation.

Joobs provide a multi-purpose utility service. They serve for drinking-water, for culinary purposes, as public bathing places, as communal latrines, for washing domestic linen and utensils, for carrying off the refuse, including the carcasses of cats, dogs and rats, as well as for irrigating the fields and gardens.

Like his Roman counterpart Balbus, who spent his time building walls, Ali has just dug a *joob*, is in the act of digging one, or is about to begin digging one. And as with the beavers in a North American valley the signs of his activities are everywhere, even on the main highway itself.

So it happened that on our drive from Qazvin to Tabriz, progress was retarded by frequent slow-downs to cross *joobs*. Most of them were mere saucer-like depressions, and we slowed down and drove straight through them with a pleasant switch-back sensation. But some of the deeper ones could be treacherous and called for a different approach. If not too wide the most effective way was to step on the accelerator and take them in one's stride.

I had been using the cautious approach all the morning with complete success, until we came upon a super-*joob*. This *joob*-digger had done a really thorough job and must have been working all night on it. His *joob* was both deep and wide, but the edges were so cleanly cut that I did not see it until I was actually in it.

The front wheels went down with a bang and a crash which shook the whole car. There goes our front axle, I thought. But Allah was merciful, and with much lugging and tugging we managed to get Zobeida out. Then we got to work with the shovel which I had brought all the way from Beirut, but not yet used, and we tackled the *joob*. When we finished, its usefulness as a *joob* was doubtful, but the road was once again open, and the farther we got from Qazvin the fewer *joobs* we encountered.

This part of the country that we were now traversing had from very early times been the homeland of a brave and warlike highland tribal people, the Dailamites, whose raids and depredations upon the towns and settled districts further south had made them greatly feared throughout the whole of that part of Iran. Qazvin, in particular, was the frequent victim of their hostile attentions, which continued throughout several centuries, during which on at least one occasion Qazvin was actually captured and occupied.

When, in AD 641, the Moslem Arab invaders swept into north-west Iran, the Dailamites put up a prolonged and bitter resistance, and it was not for nearly three centuries that the Dailamite power was finally broken, and the tribespeople were converted to Islam. However, the compulsory change of religion did not diminish the warlike character of the Dailamite people and it was not long before trouble again broke out in this wild mountainous country.

At a point along the road, some seventy kilometres from Qazvin, we could see a range of bare hills rising in the middle distance and through glasses I could discern one outstanding rocky mass. From its location I was satisfied that this must be the famous Rock of Alamut on which stood the tenth-century castle which for nearly two hundred years was the stronghold of the Order of the Assassins.

The trouble began in AD 1090, when an extremely able leader of the Ismaili sect of Shiah Moslems named Hassan-es-Sabbah led a revolt against the ruling Sunni faction. The revolt had been well planned and resulted in the capture of a number of key strongholds strategically located in Iran and Syria. One of these fortresses was Alamut, situated on a precipitous rock overlooking a valley. Hassan-es-Sabbah made Alamut the headquarters of a new order which he called the Order of the Hashishin, or Hashish-Eaters, or, as their arch-enemies the Crusaders phonetically misnamed them, the Assassins.

Being essentially a militant order, the Grand Master's first step was to recruit a striking force of *fida'i*, or Devoted Ones, from among the young men of the Dailamite and other warlike hill tribes, with a special eye to their physique and toughness of character. They were put through a rigorous course of what today would be called commando training, aimed at proficiency in gaining access to Crusader and other enemy strongholds, preparatory to their capture by surprise attack. These methods were so successful that one great fortress after another fell to the forces of the *fida'i*, whose training was also directed towards the systematic liquidation of the Grand Master's political enemies by murder, or, as it now came to be known—by assassination.

The Devoted Ones were especially expert in the art of stabbing with the dagger or strangling with the bowstring. It is believed that the one thing the training curriculum neglected was proficiency in making a subsequent escape, it being assumed that opportunity for such action would rarely, if ever, present itself.

As part of the general scheme of operation, the Grand Master had a beautiful park-like garden laid out in the fertile Alamut valley, with an abundance of trees, flowering shrubs, fountains and, most important, a bevy of damsels of outstanding charm and beauty. It was in conjunction with this garden that the eating of hashish played its important role.

After concluding their training and before being despatched on an assignment, the Devoted Ones were drugged with hashish and were taken to the garden. There, after recovering consciousness, they were allowed to spend several days dallying with the lovely maidens, in what to them appeared nothing less than Paradise. After this, they were again drugged, and awoke to find themselves back in the grim, prison-like fortress of Alamut.

Now came the pay-off. Each youth would be called up before the Grand Master and asked if he had enjoyed his stay in the garden. On hearing his enthusiastic reply that it had been a paradise on earth, the Grand Master would smile benignly and say 'All right, my boy. Now you go and slay so-and-so,' and he would designate some important individual whom he wished removed. 'If you kill him, I shall have you instantly transferred to the *real* Paradise, where everything, particularly the girls, will be one thousand times better than where you have just been. Should you perish in the attempt, you will assuredly go there, all the same. So fear nothing, you'll get your reward anyway.'

The simple youths would cheerfully embark on their murderous mission and the genial old Sheikh would rub his hands gleefully, as he crossed out the name of one more enemy and another of the Devoted Ones from his list.

The system worked so well that stronghold after stronghold fell to the followers of the order. Meanwhile, more and more castles were built, wherever possible in strategic positions commanding a main route or valley, until ultimately a network of magnificent fortresses and outposts gave the Assassins control over a vast territory from the Syrian coast in the west to the borders of Afghanistan in the east.

Subsequently, Hassan-es-Sabbah was succeeded as Grand Master by the Sheikh-el-Jebel, the Old Man of the Mountain. Under the rule of the Sheikh, the order acquired its greatest political influence. The Crusaders in their castles had good reason to fear its ruthless efficiency, and the name of the Old

Man of the Mountain became legendary throughout Europe, while in the territories directly dominated by the order the leaders of the orthodox Sunni sect lived in constant dread of assassination, until it seemed that the entire Moslem religious structure might be subjugated by this extremely fanatical political organisation.

Finally, after over a century and a half, the reign of terror came to a violent end in AD 1258, when the Mongol hordes of Hulagu swept down from the north and systematically destroyed the innumerable Assassin strongholds throughout the vast territory they had dominated.

The movement was shattered and its followers dispersed. A number made their way to India, where their descendants have long since established reputable Ismaili communities. The spiritual leader of the sect is today the Agha Khan. In Iran, especially in the region bordering on the Afghan frontier between Birjand and Turbet, there still exist numerous Ismaili communities, and years before I had the pleasure of visiting one of them near the town of Qain in the company of a nephew of the late Agha Khan. We, or rather the nephew, received a most enthusiastic welcome. The villagers insisted on kissing his boots and entertained us lavishly at a feast for which, in lieu of the fatted calf, they sacrificed a couple of fat-tailed sheep.

Continuing our journey, a few miles further on we came to Khurruṃdereh, a village prettily situated on a stream and surrounded by poplar and willow trees. There was of course a *chae-khaneh*, and we stopped for a lunch of *churek* and hard-boiled eggs and the inevitable glass of tea.

As we were just starting off again, a couple of *charvadars* came along with a string of mules, greeted us and paused for a chat. I asked them how far it was to Sultaniyeh. One of them took off his pudding-bowl headgear, scratched his greasy mat of hair, and after a moment's hesitation said it would be seven *farsang*. His companion contradicted him, and said it would be about five. We split the difference, and six *farsang* proved about correct, assuming the *farsang* to be roughly five kilometres.

Like the *kos* in India, the Iranian *farsang* (or *farsakh*) is apt to be a very elastic term, and varies with the individual's sense of distance, or lack of it, but also with the nature of the ground, being longer when the road is good and shorter when it is bad. This is understandable, since one popular definition of a *farsang* is the distance covered in one hour by a good horse at a walking pace.

It was not long afterwards that we sighted a large dome and knew that we were approaching Sultaniyeh. As we came within a few hundred yards of it a slanting silvery ray of sunshine broke through the heavy cloud masses and shone directly down upon the dome and its immediate surroundings, so that they stood out vivid and golden against the sombre background.

Unfortunately my camera had become buried under the baggage, and by the time I had retrieved it the sun was again obscured and the whole effect had vanished. I had missed a most striking picture.

The building with the dome is the fourteenth-century mausoleum of Oljeitu (AD 1304–17), brother and successor to the Mongol El-Khan Ghazal (AD 1295–1304), whose capital city was Tabriz. In its prime the mausoleum must have been an architectural masterpiece and a work of great beauty.

The huge dome is elongated, almost egg-shaped, and rests on a tall, two-storeyed octagon, having three arches on each side of the upper storey, and a minaret at each of the eight corners. Originally the dome was encased in shiny blue-green tilework and, glistening in the sunlight, it would have been a striking landmark for many kilometres around. Now much of the tilework had fallen away, although some parts of the interior were still covered with it, while fragments lay scattered among the soil and debris immediately surrounding the mausoleum.

There are two other old shrines in the vicinity, much smaller and less pretentious than that of the Mongol ruler. Judged by the fine brickwork, particularly of the larger of them, they must have dated from around the same period.

Abdul was unable to tell me anything about their history, but he scouted around and soon reappeared with an old gentleman who had the brightest of red beards I had ever seen. After the usual greetings he told me his name was Ghulam Hussein and that he was the guardian of the shrines. He said the larger one was the tomb of one Sultan Cheilabi, and the other of Mullah Hassan. He was quite hazy about dates, but assured me they were both very ancient. I asked why nothing was being done to restore, or at least preserve, the great dome, but he merely shrugged and gave the stock reply, '*Che arz kunam.*'

From Sultaniyeh the road continued for some distance across the flat stony plain, which despite appearances was steadily rising, to Zinjan, 5,500 feet above sea-level. The town is attractively situated among hills through which the stream, the Zinjan Rud, flows in a northerly direction. Gardens with willow and poplar trees relieve the surrounding bareness, but apart from a couple of blue-domed tombs, there appeared to be nothing of architectural or historic merit to justify our halting.

Lower downstream at the village of Nekbag there was a fine Shah Abbas caravanserai, and at another village beyond that quite a number of caravanserais. These seemed to indicate a considerable volume of road traffic coming down from Tabriz and the Caucasus.

Beyond this point the river carved its course through a range of hills and further on we crossed the stream by an unusually fine bridge.

Now began the long ascent of the Kafkan Kuh, and the only really difficult part of the whole journey. I had been warned to expect trouble at this stage, for until recently the road had been nothing more than a mule track, but I was told it had now been widened sufficiently for wheeled traffic. As we began the long climb I could see signs of widening, but the work had been so miserably carried out that in a number of places I only succeeded in manoeuvring Zobeida across after both Abdul and I had set to work collecting piles of rocks and pieces of boulder with which we built up the track.

We reached the summit with Zobeida's radiator spouting steam like a locomotive, and ourselves puffing and panting from our combined pushing and roadmaking exertions. The descent on the northern slope was even more tortuous and troublesome than the ascent, and we arrived at the bottom equally breathless.

Mianeh is considerably lower than Zinjan, a mere 3,800 feet above sea-level. The river flows past it and as at Zinjan the town is surrounded with willows and poplars. The only item of interest that I saw was a tomb with a blue dome, and I might have stopped to photograph this had it not been for Abdul.

He had admitted to ignorance about this part of the country and had been unusually silent most of the way from Qazvin. Such conversation as he had made had been confined to disparaging comments on the general character of the inhabitants, whose customs, general appearance and language he described as *wahshi*, which means uncouth, savage, barbaric, and a lot more unpleasant terms all rolled into one.

He now urged me not to dawdle at Mianeh. 'Why not?' I asked.

'Because, Agha, the bugs are very bad.'

'But aren't they bad everywhere?' I said, and then I remembered a story about the xenophobic bugs of Mianeh, how they were exceedingly voracious and hostile to any stranger, but lived on terms of peaceful coexistence with the local natives.

Abdul now amplified the story. 'These particular bugs,' he explained, 'were called *mala*, and their bite was deadly poison. Fortunately they were only found in Mianeh and its immediate neighbourhood. One day, a long time ago, a local villager was killed in a quarrel by a man from a more distant village called Hashtrud. While the corpse lay ready for burial, a *djinn* got inside it, and out of its mouth there came a large number of *mala*. They got loose and swarmed into Mianeh. Through the years they multiplied, and whenever they scented a man from Hashtrud, they would attack him, and the man always died. Even today the *mala* still remember the bloodfeud and if they bite a Hashtrudi, he quickly dies.'

'But don't they bite other people as well?' I asked.

'Surely, Agha, but they do not die; they only get very ill.'

'Let's get out of here,' I said quickly, so we drove on, and I did not get a photograph of the shrine with the blue dome.

There was a pleasant interlude on the last lap of the trip. Away on the left, within a short distance of the road, was a stretch of marshland bordering on a large lake. It came as an agreeable change after the arid landscape. I could see some duck on the water well out of gunshot, but the marsh looked like promising snipe ground.

I habitually carried a shotgun with me on these long journeys, both for possible small game and also for protection. Now I welcomed the chance to stretch my legs, so got out the gun and a few cartridges and began walking up the reed-covered marsh. Within the first five minutes I flushed a snipe and promptly collected him. I walked on some distance, but saw no more birds, so put the snipe in the back of the car and packed away the gun.

In Tabriz I was warmly welcomed by Charlie Stevens. He had been British Consular Representative there for many years and was popular with Iranians and Europeans alike. He was also famous for his hospitality.

'Of course you're going to stay with me, and you're just in time for tea,' he greeted me, and after a quick wash and brush-up, I found myself in a pleasant sitting room, enjoying some delicious tea and buttered toast. So warm was the welcome and so interesting the conversation, that it was only that evening at dinner-time that I remembered the snipe.

'By the way,' I said, 'I passed a biggish marsh some way back along the road. It looked likely snipe ground and . . .'

'Yes,' Charlie broke in, 'I know the place. Good duck shooting in winter, but snipe . . . d'you know, it's a strange thing, but there's only one single snipe there. He's been there for years, and he's quite a famous bird. In fact, a bit of a legend has grown up around him, and there's a belief among the local Iranians here that he's a *djinn* in bird form, and that nobody can shoot him. The whole of the European community have had shots at him one time or another, and I myself have potted at him lots of times. He certainly has a charmed life, but I don't believe in *djinn* and I'll get him one of these days.'

I felt painfully embarrassed and there was a momentary silence. Charlie sensed it and caught my look. 'What?' he said. 'No, you don't mean to say . . .?' He glared at me.

'Yes,' I confessed, 'I'm afraid I did. I had no idea . . . I'm terribly sorry.'

Charlie, good fellow, broke into a grin. 'The only snipe in Azerbaijan! We even called him *Zahid*, the hermit. I was getting quite fond of that bird. Anyway, he'll come in nicely for your breakfast.'

But it was Charlie who ate Zahid. I insisted on that.

Charlie Stevens was not only a wonderful host, but also a veritable mine of information on a wide range of subjects. He enjoyed friendly relations with Iranian officialdom from the Governor downwards, and in addition had a host of Iranian friends in both business and social circles. I met a number of these and learned a great deal from them and from one prominent merchant in particular. He gave me valuable information regarding the import and export trade with the Caucasus and was well informed about conditions in Iran generally. I told him the places I had seen, and mentioned Qazvin. He shrugged deprecatingly. A waste of time, he said. The Qazvins were very small people and were not interested in anything outside their own bazaar. I would do better to stay a few days longer in Tabriz and miss Qazvin. I took his advice, remained a whole week in Tabriz and found it well worth while.

Chapter 8

TABRIZ

As the capital of Iranian Azerbaijan and second largest city in the country, Tabriz fell very short of my expectations. I had hoped for something more impressive in the way of general layout and public buildings, and also for more surviving ancient monuments. But I was forgetting two vital factors which have periodically plagued Tabriz throughout its long, eventful history. These are, firstly that the city lies directly on the invasion route from the north and secondly, that it also lies in an active earthquake belt. Between invasions and earthquakes, with occasional epidemics of plague and cholera, Tabriz has had a very chequered history.

Strangely enough the Mongol invaders, who devastated most of the rest of Iran, spared Tabriz. On two occasions their hordes reached the city's gates but allowed themselves to be bought off, and when they did subsequently take possession of it, instead of destroying it as was their wont, they made it their centre of government and capital of an empire extending from the Nile to the Oxus. In fact they gave Tabriz its Golden Age.

There must have been some strange quirk in the Mongol leaders which brought about a radical change in their temperament and behaviour in the course of a few decades. In AD 1258 their hordes had swept through Iran with a bestial savagery equalled only by Attila and his Huns eight centuries earlier. In their lust for conquest, they laid themselves out to destroy every vestige of civilisation and culture. Yet within a mere four decades, the Mongol El-Khan Ghazan (1295–1304) was embellishing Tabriz with a wealth of fine buildings, including an enormous royal mausoleum and extensive bazaars. Under his rule the city also became a famous centre of learning.

Ghazan's brother and successor, Oljaitu, whose tomb we saw at Sultaniyeh, continued the work of embellishment, and it was during his reign that the enormous mosque, the Masjid-e-Shah 'Ali, was built.

After the collapse of the Mongol dynasty, few outstanding monuments were erected, and only portions of two of them have survived to the present day. One is the Blue Mosque, built by Shah Jehan of the 'Black Sheep' Turkmen dynasty, who ruled 1436–1467. Of the mosque, little more than one of its entrance portals, now in dilapidated condition, is still standing. Sufficient of the original tilework remains to convey an impression of the colourful appearance of the structure in its prime, but most of the masonry at the base of the arch has been eroded or filched by local stone robbers and unless something was done very soon to repair the damage, the archway's days were clearly numbered.

The second ancient monument is the surviving portion of the great Masjid-e-Shah 'Ali, much of which was destroyed at different times by earthquakes, though sufficient still remains to give an idea of its enormous size.

A third, and the most imposing, public monument is the Arg or Citadel. It can hardly be called ancient, because although it originally formed part of the great Masjid, most of it was reconstructed and converted to its present use as recently as 1809. Since then, however, it has earned a sinister reputation, like the ancient Tower of Death in Old Bokhara, for the number of criminals and political offenders, not to mention faithless wives and surplus concubines, flung from its summit.

There is a well-known story of a certain lady who was launched into space in the usual manner, but whose wide heavy skirts belled out and parachuted her safely to earth. One would like to think—though the story does not say so—that the Governor was so impressed by this manifestation of divine protection that he gave the lady a free pardon, but in the light of other known cases, it is much more probable that his curiosity impelled him to order her to do it again.

Then there was the tragic case of the Bab, the spiritual

head of the Bahai Sect. On that occasion too, back in 1830, a miracle happened. The Bab and certain of this followers, likewise condemned to death, were first suspended by ropes slung beneath their armpits, and then executed by firing-squad. After the smoke from the volley had cleared away, the riddled corpses of his followers hung there for all to see. But the Bab himself had disappeared.

For a few moments the onlookers stood aghast. Startled true-believers plucked at their beards and invoked Allah. Wah! Wah! A miracle! The bullets of the executioners had flown high and had neatly severed the rope. That surely was a manifestation of divine protection. But the next moment the Bab was found hiding in a guard room. He was promptly strung up again and this time there was no miracle. When the smoke cleared away, his riddled body was hanging with the others.

The Tabriz bazaars are of the enclosed pattern, built on the same model as those of Tehran and Isfahan. Here are the mysterious labyrinths of long dark passages, dependent for illumination upon apertures in the lofty vaulted roof. Shafts of sunlight pierced the clouds of dust, stirred up and held in suspension by the constant movement of the milling throng, and appearing as golden columns in the surrounding semi-darkness.

The main passages have numerous narrower ones branching off them, and all are lined on either side by a continuous row of shops and stalls. Most of these are little more than cubicles, about twenty feet square, but many of them have a second cubicle as store-room or office in the rear and in some cases these in turn open onto a paved courtyard or even into a full-size caravanserai, where the merchandise is carried in and off-loaded from the caravan or pack animals, literally in the merchant's own backyard.

The dealers themselves squat cross-legged on the rug-covered floors of their shops, which are generally raised a couple of feet or more above the level of the alleyway. From this commanding position they are within arm's reach and greeting distance of the passing throng. They spend most of their day in this sedentary position, their gaze vacant and distant, like Buddhist monks or Hindu sadhus in a posture of placid contemplation. But appearances are deceptive; their eyes are keen and they are wide awake, ready and alert like birds of prey, to pounce upon any potential victim.

On entering the bazaars from the brilliant sunshine one's first impression is that of a madhouse, in which the lighting system has suddenly failed and the inmates are on the rampage. Then, as one's eyes grow accustomed to the dim half-light and one's ears to the clamour, so one's nose is assailed by the bewildering variety of smells. That of spices usually predominates, and blends rather well with a background bouquet of camel-dung laced with charcoal fumes. To these add the nauseating reek of damp, half-cured leather, molten mutton-fat, and sweating human bodies, the pungent smell of garlic and asafoetida, and the aromas of musk, incense and cedar-wood, and the final result is that indefinable yet unmistakable something which, whether in Cairo, Tehran or Marrakesh, can only be described as plain 'bazaar smell'.

As for the crowds which frequent the bazaars, they represent a cross-section of the population of the particular region. But as I see them they fall into three main classes: children, people from the outside world, and the permanent denizens of these vaulted market places.

I am always filled with pity for the children, particularly the bazaar- and city-bred youngsters. So very many of them, despite their grimy faces and verminous ragged garments, are really beautiful, or would be if one could take them home and scrub them. Most pitiable of all, I think, are the children of metal-workers, scarcely more than toddlers, who ought to be playing in the sunshine. Instead, they are condemned to crouch in perpetual twilight, their puny hands clutching full-size hammers, as hour after hour they beat out sheets of brass or copper. They are in the process of initiation into a merciless lifelong drudgery. Other trades are equally strenuous, that of the carpet-weavers, for example, but the child metal-workers always arouse my deepest pity.

Yet it is the crowds from the outside world who provide the real life and colour, movement and vitality of the bazaars. They carry in with them an element of sunlight and fresh air, dispelling the gloom and enlivening the atmosphere of these cellar-like surroundings. Without them the bazaars would be completely dead. As for the permanent residents of this sunless underworld—the craftsmen, merchants, brokers, pedlars and countless underlings and parasites—they again are something quite apart with their pale, bloodless faces and their flabby arms, like the nameless white creatures found squirming under rocks when one suddenly turns them over.

It is an unpleasing comparison and a very unfair one, for what can be expected of people who spend the greater part of their lives, from earliest childhood, in a dust-laden atmosphere, deafening clamour and perpetual semi-darkness. Poor devils! Life can hold little lustre for them.

As I picked my way through the crowded alleyways, the jostling, shouting throng swirled and eddied around and behind me, leaving me helpless as a piece of flotsam carried by the current. In the incessant clamour, the ear was slow to pick out individual sounds. Frantic shouts of *Khabardar*! Look out! close behind me failed to register. Next moment I ducked quickly, as a grotesque, foul-smelling, hairy head brushed my shoulder and slobbered in my ear. I side-stepped promptly onto the next man's toes and flattened myself against a pillar to avoid being crushed by a whole string of camels, laden with enormous bales of merchandise, which filled up the entire fairway.

Hardly had they passed, when another shout of *Khabardar*! immediately to my rear was followed by a donkey ramming his head into the small of my back, and half a dozen overloaded little beasts, impelled by whacks and maledictions (ohé, ye sons of burnt fathers!) forced a passage through the jam-packed alleyway.

I explored the Tabriz bazaars in quest of material for my

report, rather than to make purchases. But my search resulted in my acquiring an article of great beauty. I had groped my way through the densely packed quarter of the cloth-merchants and had reached a point in the rabbit warren of alleyways where a shaft of dazzling sunlight cut through the enveloping gloom and lit up the immediate surroundings like a powerful spotlight in a circus arena.

I thought of a circus rather than a theatre because, standing in the full radiance of the beam of golden light was the biggest and finest milk-white donkey I have ever seen. He was a noble beast, and he seemed to know it. A pure-blooded Bahreini, I guessed, and I paused to admire him. I gave him a friendly pat on the neck and from the animal itself my gaze then wandered to the brightly coloured *zinposh* or saddle-cloth which covered his back and rump. The colours glistened in the sunlight, and I could see that the *zinposh* was an unusually good specimen, with an exceptionally fine stitch and pattern.

Observing my interest, the donkey's owner, whom I had not noticed at first, as he was standing in the shadow, now came forward and greeted me. He was an elderly man with a henna-dyed red beard, a twinkle in his eyes, and a shrewd and calculating smile on his thin lips. He looked a pleasant, but tough character.

He opened up with: '*Khub ast, nakhair*, Agha? A fine one, isn't it?'

I agreed that it was *kheili khub*, very fine.

'Would your Honour not like to purchase it?' The question sprang readily to his lips.

'That,' I said, 'depends on how much you want for it.'

He stroked his red beard pensively for a moment, threw me a shrewd glance, and named me a sum out of all proportion.

I said jokingly, 'Why I could buy the donkey itself for that price.'

He looked surprised.

'But don't you want the donkey, Agha?'

Then without waiting for a reply, he let himself go in a long panegyric of the animal's merits. Never had there been such a prince of a beast: he was as speedy as a racehorse and as gentle as a gazelle. In short, he was the very pearl of an *oolagh* (ass).

I tried to make the old gentleman understand that I did not want the donkey. All I was interested in was the *zinposh*.

'The *zinposh*!' He mumbled the word, and a look of bewilderment came over his face. He went off again in a flurry of argument, assuring me that however good the donkey I already had, it could not possible equal this one. I should therefore do well, he argued, to sell my present beast and buy this prince of all *oolaghs*.

'But I don't have a donkey. I don't need a donkey,' I protested.

Now he looked really perplexed. But if I didn't have a donkey and didn't need a donkey, why in the name of Allah did I need a *zinposh*? It just did not make sense.

'All right,' I said in a tone of finality. 'If you don't want to sell, it's of no importance.' I made as if to go away.

'Wait!' said the old man. 'After all, it's not my business what you do with the *zinposh*. I'll let you have it for . . .' The sum he mentioned was on the high side, but not exorbitantly so, and obviously a counter-offer was expected.

By this time the usual crowd had collected. The ball was momentarily on my side of the net, and all eyes were on me.

With a friendly smile I reminded my opponent that we were discussing a mere *zinposh* and not a full-size *ghali* (carpet) or even a prayer-rug, and, I added for emphasis only, it was only a *zinposh* for a donkey and not even for a horse!

The shrewd old eyes twinkled, but his lips remained pressed tight.

'*W'allah*, but *what* a donkey! Is he not as big as a horse?' He turned for affirmation to the crowd, and a chorus of Wah! Wah! broke out in support.

'However,' he went on, 'since the Agha is evidently not wealthy and does not even possess a donkey, then we must be generous. Give me . . . krans, Agha, and the *zinposh* is yours.'

'*W'allah*, Agha,' I said, 'truly you are so fair-minded that I will step up my offer and we will split the difference.' To this he agreed, and we concluded the deal.

But the old man was still not satisfied. He had something on his mind.

'By the Holy Imam, Agha,' he said, 'you *feringhis* are strange people. My brother who lives in Isfahan owns an old *ambar*, a barn. It is very old and in ancient times it was part of a caravanserai. In proof of its age it had a stone over the big doorway with an inscription, but it was written in some ancient script which none could read. One day, a *feringhi*, an Amerikani, came to my brother and offered to buy the stone with the inscription. But my brother would not sell the stone, though he was willing to sell the whole barn. They argued for a long time and finally agreed a price, and the Amerikani bought the whole barn. Then he got a mason and removed the stone. 'This is all I want,' he said. 'You can keep the barn!'

Wah! Wah! came a murmur from the crowd. 'Truly the *feringhi* was afflicted,' concluded the old man, 'for what could he do with one single stone without the barn? And what can you do, Agha, with a *zinposh* without a donkey?'

Chapter 9

THE MANJIL PASS

I was very reluctant to leave Charlie Stevens' hospitable roof, but although he pressed me to stay longer, I had to think of the long journey ahead; also I felt I had imbibed as much vodka as was good for me.

I had spent some time the previous day going over Zobeida with a grease-gun and spanner. I changed the oil, checked the tyres and made sure she was roadworthy. Next morning broke fair, the weather had turned slightly warmer and there was even a touch of spring in the air. The open road beckoned and, after an early breakfast and with a well-filled luncheon basket, we set off. I had abandoned my plan to return via Maragha, as road conditions were said to be atrocious, and would return by the road we had come by as far as Qazvin, and then head north for Resht and Pahlevi.

We hurried past Mianeh as we remembered the story of the xenophobic bugs. We again had a stiff climb over the Kaflan Kuh, but thanks to our road-making efforts on the outward journey we completed the ascent without difficulty, and found the southern descent easier than expected.

For want of a better place I spent the night at the Qazvin Hotel and was lucky in getting a room to myself. I had a meal in the restaurant—eating-house would better describe it—then turned in early because there was nothing else to do, and after the late nights at Tabriz I needed to catch up on my sleep.

It was pleasing to hear the local people talking Persian again, instead of the less agreeable Turkish dialect which we had been hearing throughout Azerbaijan. There was a friendlier feeling in the air too, and despite the lack of facilities and the primitive conditions in the Qazvin Hotel, one felt that one was back in a cultured country.

We made an early start and headed due north for Manjil, in the open valley, before entering the mountainous region of Mazenderan.

'Manjil is the windiest place in the whole country,' Abdul warned me, 'and when the wind blows from a certain quarter, all the snakes come out and collect in the valley.'

'Why do they do that?' I asked.

'*Che arz kunam.* Perhaps to eat the air.' Abdul was rarely at a loss for a reply. Repartee, or *hazir-jawabi* as the Persians call it, is greatly esteemed in this country. (In Persian *hawa khurdan*, to eat the air, means to enjoy the fresh air.)

It was indeed very windy at Manjil, just as Abdul had predicted, but we saw no snakes (this was not the right wind, he explained). As we headed north to the Caspian, we followed the course of the Safeed Rud into the deep and narrow valley formed by the lofty spurs of the Pusht-i-Kuh on our left hand and the steep slopes of the Kuh-i-Darfak, a terminal cross-spur of the main Elburz range, on our right. The mountain slopes, drab, arid and treeless, with their higher ridges buried in heavy cloud, closed in on us until the valley became a gorge and the road a rocky track.

Somewhere behind those cloud-wreathed ranges lay the dense forest belt of Gilan and Mazanderan, the haunt of the Hyrcanean tiger. I knew that I must be already on the outskirts of the forest, but so far there was not a sign to suggest its existence. I had read of the abrupt transition in this area from bare hills to lush rain-forest, but I never expected anything so startling as the contrast proved to be.

We continued along a roughly made road, badly rutted and covered with a deep layer of sandy grit. We had a following wind blowing up the gorge, carrying clouds of dust ahead of us. The car was full of it and so was our clothing and our nostrils. We could not see clearly in front of us. Then suddenly came the change. We rounded a sharp bend and were in a totally different country.

In less time than it takes to write this, we had moved from the dry, stony track to a grass-bordered lane, inches deep in heavy greasy mud. The higher slopes of the mountains were covered with thick forest and enveloped in rolling banks of dark-grey cloud, while rain was falling with gentle persistence. From the deep mud on the road and the sodden state of vegetation, it seemed to have been raining for months.

The road itself was just sufficiently wide for two cars to pass with very few inches to spare. On our left, the jungle-clad mountainside rose sternly from the road itself, but on our right there was a ditch of sorts, masked by long grass and backed by a thick tangle of bushes and tree branches. It looked exactly like an overgrown English hedge.

I had been too occupied trying to prevent the front wheels skidding on the greasy road surface to pay attention to the bushes at the side, but from somewhere far down below one could hear the muffled roar of a torrent, and subconsciously one was aware that the mountainside must fall away abruptly into the gorge.

As we approached the next bend we heard the sound of jingling bells. I expected a mule train, but suddenly there came into view four horses harnessed abreast to the leading *fourgon* of a whole line of Russian wagons.

In a moment the narrow road seemed completely full of prancing horses, evidently unused to motor cars and showing extreme nervousness.

There was clearly no room in the road for us to pass, and for the *fourgons* to turn round and go back was out of the question. I did what I thought in the circumstances was the only practical thing. I steered the car to the right edge of the road and deliberately ditched it. That is to say, I purposely let the off-wheels slide into what I fully believed was just an ordinary ditch, at the most a foot deep.

But I was wrong, terribly, dangerously wrong. As the right front wheel and then the right rear wheel left the road and sank into the grass, and the car dipped over, a most frightening thing happened.

Instead of tilting just a few inches, Zobeida gave a lurch,

dipped over a full forty-five degrees, and then began slowly to slide sideways and downwards. In that moment I realised with a shock that what I had thought was an ordinary roadside ditch overgrown with grass, was actually no ditch at all, but the edge of the precipice. The bushes and branches which had all the appearance of a hedge were growing out of the side of the cliff.

The natural impulse was to jump out as quickly as possible, but this was impossible for several reasons. First of these was the steep angle at which we were tilted. Secondly, as a result of the strain on the chassis and body, the door by the driver's seat had become jammed, and the rear door could not be opened because it had a bundle of bedding roped on outside. Thirdly, we also realised that the slightest movement might send the car hurtling over the edge into the gorge hundreds of feet below.

I heard Abdul hurriedly invoking the name of Allah over and over again, but to do him justice he kept his head and did not move. Actually, the suspense only lasted for minutes, though to me it seemed interminable as one after the other, we very very slowly and carefully climbed out through the window over the jammed door. Only when we were safely out of the car could we really appreciate the narrowness of our escape. While the bushes and tree branches concealed the edge of the precipice from view, the two right wheels had actually slipped over the edge and were hanging with nothing beneath them but a sheer drop into the gorge.

The brushwood was not sufficiently strong to have offered any resistance. Zobeida was literally hanging by the left front wheel and by the differential housing on the back axle. This had caught on the very brink of the cliff and mercifully held us.

When we grasped the actual situation, we just looked at each other without uttering a word, but there was no doubt in our minds that God in that moment had been very near.

We dared not touch the car. The drivers of the *fourgons* were Tatars from Azerbaijan, and a surly crowd. They had meanwhile guided their animals and carts past us, and without a thought to our trouble they went on their way. We lost sight of them round a bend in the road and the sound of their harness-bells died away in the distance.

If Abdul's maledictions could have produced results, then a cloud of smoke should have marked their passing, as he scorched and carbonised the fathers of all Tatars in general, and those *fourgon*-drivers in particular.

I left Abdul to enlist the help of any chance wayfarers, and myself trudged through the rain and mud to a wayside village we had passed about half a mile back. I was lucky to find the headman and told him of our trouble. He quickly rounded up a dozen villagers and collected ropes. Very very carefully we roped the two wheels which still held the ground, and with great difficulty we secured more ropes round the two outside wheels. We were taking no chances, for the least movement could have sent the car over the edge. We fastened still more ropes round the front and rear axle. Then we all hauled together and by sheer force pulled Zobeida back onto the road.

I have never paid our silver krans with greater readiness and gratitude. The villagers were happy and so were we, but as we started up the engine and went on our way, I joined with Abdul in mentally burning the fathers of all four-horse *fourgons*.

The incident with the Tatars had lost us a full two hours and now, with our slow rate of progress along the narrow slippery road, we would not reach Resht until after dark. I had been invited to stay with the Vice-Consul, and he had written to me, strongly urging me to reach there before nightfall. The road, he warned, was very bad in places and difficult to negotiate in the dark, also there was always the chance of being held up and robbed.

The air was warm and clammy. I had got very wet walking back to the village, and at intervals I found myself sneezing. Each time this happened I heard a muttered *bism'illah* from Abdul.

It began to get dark early in the afternoon. The rain showed no sign of letting up, and the clouds hung like a dark heavy shroud over the tops of the trees. Of the hillsides themselves nothing was visible. Only the water gushed in scores of rivulets gurgling and bubbling as it splashed down the moss- and herbage-covered face of rock, and streamed in runnels and channels across the road and over the grass-concealed brink beyond. Meanwhile, like a constant threat or warning, the muffled roar of the torrent was always in our ears. We kept away from the edge.

Soon it got so dark that we needed headlights, and now we met with our second setback. Our lights failed to function. The rain might have had something to do with it, but more likely the great strain on the chassis as it was hauled back onto the road had damaged the circuit. Whatever the cause, the lights refused to work. I fiddled about with the wiring in the dusk and pouring rain and finally gave it up. There was nothing for it. We would have to finish the journey in the dark without lights.

Abdul, of course, had his explanation. 'Did not this slave make petition that trouble would happen?' was his polite way of saying 'I told you so.' I had sneezed so many times, the engine must be choked with *djinn*.

Fortunately, we met no more *fourgons*, but we experienced a few tense moments at a particularly narrow portion of the gorge where the track disappeared abruptly round the cliff-face. We were still some fifty paces short of the bend when we saw a faint glow which threw up the outline of the cliff in silhouette. The glow became rapidly brighter, and I pulled over as close as I dared to the outside edge and jammed on the brakes hard to lock the car.

Next moment a blaze of light almost blinded us as the approaching vehicle rounded the bend and its glaring head-lights shone straight into our faces.

It was travelling far too fast for safety, but the driver saw us just in time and cleared us by inches. Next moment he was followed by a second car which shaved us even closer. There were five cars in all. They did not slacken speed, nor did they even sound their horns. In the blinding glare we could not see who or what they were. I felt certain that they were a Soviet trade mission on its way to Tehran. We had heard rumours that one was expected.

'But why travel by night?' I wondered.

Abdul shrugged. 'When do the Reds ever do anything openly? They probably have good reasons for not wanting to be seen.'

The rain poured down in a continuous tropical deluge as we bumped and splashed along a road deep in mud. It was already late when we reached Resht, to find an anxious Vice-Consul awaiting me with drinks, a hot bath and an appetising dinner.

The next morning the rain had ceased, but the sky remained heavily overcast, and a thick mist added to the general gloom. Further on it became less misty and we could see buffaloes ploughing up the mud in the paddy-fields, and women bent nearly double planting out the young rice seedlings. The whole scene was vividly reminiscent of Burma or Ceylon, or almost anywhere in the Orient, and seemed to follow as a natural sequence to the lush rain-forest we had now left behind us.

We drove on to Pahlevi just to get a glimpse of the Caspian, but found the view very depressing. Two Soviet vessels were tied up alongside a ramshackle wooden pier. One was a small freighter, the other a naval gunboat. Both had a neglected appearance, and badly needed a coat of paint. The red flag with the hammer and sickle drooped mournfully from their sterns. Probably the Soviet trade mission whose wild nocturnal dash had given us such a close shave, had landed from one of these vessels.

I caused a flutter on board by photographing the gunboat. Several persons on her deck shouted and waved their arms. I waved back, then turned and walked away.

The caviare industry, I learned, was passing through a slack period. Originally the Russians had held a local caviare concession, but with the revolution this had fallen into abeyance, and it was said that the Soviets were currently trying to persuade the Tehran Government to renew it. Possibly the trade mission had something to do with this.

There seemed to be nothing else to see in Pahlevi, so we drove back to Resht. There we found a mechanic who repaired Zobeida's lighting system, and after accepting the Vice-Consul's hospitality again for lunch, I started back with Abdul for Qazvin and Tehran, glad to escape from the enervating heat and humidity of Mazanderan.

Soon after leaving Resht, the rain started with a light drizzle, but immediately we entered the gorge it turned into a tropical downpour, with visibility down to a few metres. Driving was easier though, as I now had the right side of the road, which was flanked by a wall of rock. We encountered no wheeled traffic and I could keep well away from the precipitous side. The rain continued so long as we were in the gorge, but stopped when we came to the corner where the climate changed. We passed through the bare low-lying slopes of the foothills, and were once again on the open road, with a strong wind blowing gritty dust-clouds into our faces.

We briefly patronised a *chae-khaneh* on the outskirts of Qazvin, and then we turned eastwards on the last lap of our journey to Tehran. The road had originally been constructed by the Russians, but was now in a sorry state, owing to many years of neglect. We had a little trouble negotiating several *joobs*, especially during the first few kilometres after leaving Qazvin, and once again we had to use the spade and carry out some ditch-filling before we could proceed.

By this time the sun had broken through the clouds, but there was a chill in the air blowing straight from the snow-covered crest of the lofty Elburz range, running parallel to our road only a few kilometres to the north. Shortly afterwards the towering snow-capped cone of Demavend (18,600 ft) came into view, glistening white in the distance ahead of us, with Tehran, itself 8,750 feet above sea-level, only another half-hour away.

The number of pack animals on the road increased as we approached the city, and soon we were driving through the rather gaudy ceramic tiled archway of the Qazvin Gate, a surprisingly commonplace entrance to an imperial capital.

Chapter 10

TEHRAN

Very little is known of the origin and early history of Tehran, since for many centuries it was overshadowed by the much older and larger neighbouring city of Ray. While both places were totally destroyed in the wholesale devastation wrought by Hulagu's Mongol hordes in AD 1220, Ray never recovered, and is today merely a site covered by ruins, while Tehran subsequently came to life and even enjoyed some measure of prosperity. But it was not until 1785, when the Qajar chieftain Mohammed Khan captured the city and made it his seat of government, that Tehran became the capital of Iran. Nevertheless, as an imperial capital Tehran was relatively a parvenu, an upstart. While the Safavid monarchs, in particular the great Shah Abbas (1587–1629), were lavishing their affection upon Isfahan, planning it on a scale befitting an imperial city, endowing it with mosques and adorning it with palaces of outstanding grace and beauty, Tehran remained for long periods neglected. Some improvements were carried out by Fath-Ali Shah (1797–1834) and during the long reign of Nasir-ud-Din (1848–96) the city underwent major alterations and increased considerably in size and population. Otherwise there were few noteworthy changes until the present century.

The year 1906 saw important political developments with the establishment of the Constitution, and the Majlis, or Parliament, held its first session. But it was not until 1921, with the Qajar dynasty still on the throne in the person of Ahmad Shah, that an event occurred which was to open a new chapter in Iranian history. In that year, a soldier of dynamic energy and forceful leadership named Reza Khan, the Commander of the Persian Cossack Brigade, in despair at the general state of lawlessness throughout the country, the incompetence of the Government and the irresolute character of the Shah, decided to move in open rebellion. In February 1921 he marched his troops to Tehran and overthrew the Government. Reza Khan was appointed Commander-in-Chief and shortly afterwards became Minister of War. In 1923 he was appointed Prime Minister. That same year, the ineffectual Ahmed Shah left the country on a prolonged visit to Europe. As he was still absent in 1925, the Majlis formally declared that the Qajar dynasty had ceased to exist, and, by an overwhelming majority decreed that the constitutional sovereignty of the realm was entrusted by the people to His Imperial Majesty Reza Shah Pahlavi and to his male descendants, generation by generation.

On my arrival in Tehran, there was much talk in official circles about the new Shah's impending coronation but few signs of excitement in the city itself. The common people seemed to be taking things very quietly and going about their business as usual.

Thanks to introductions from the legation, I was able to meet a number of officials as well as prominent business people. The Minister was away in London, but my particular friend, the Commercial Attaché, pressed me to stay as his guest for as long as my plans permitted, an invitation I was very glad to accept and which greatly added to the pleasure of my sojourn in Tehran. Also it afforded me ample time to meet all kinds of tradespeople, and I spent many hours daily, seated in their offices or squatting in their serais, discussing in leisurely tempo almost anything from the import of cotton goods and export of goatskins and dried apricots, to such diverse matters as whether motor transport will eventually supplant camel and mule, and the vexed question of chemical versus vegetable dyes in the carpet-weaving industry; all this, of course, while consuming innumerable glasses of hot sweet tea, to a background accompaniment of grumbling camels, cursing mule-drivers, and the soporific bubbling of water-pipes. Meanwhile I accumulated a mass of miscellaneous notes, which I later condensed into reports for my London friends.

One of the best-informed and most interesting businessmen I met was Mohammed Ishaq. His firm had a branch office and a representative in Manchester, from whom I had brought out a letter of introduction. He was one of the biggest importers of English cotton piece-goods, but he also dealt on a large scale with the export of carpets and rugs as well as goat- and sheepskins.

Mohammed Ishaq was physically a little man in his late fifties, with regular Semitic features and shrewd twinkling eyes which seemed to look right through one. He spoke good English and fluent French and Italian, in addition to Persian. He was a chain smoker of cigarettes, though he appeared to be equally happy with the mouth-piece of a *qalian* between his lips. He was full of nervous energy—his fingers played constantly with an amber rosary of conversation-beads, and he had a habit of frequently looking around in a conspiratorial manner, as though afraid of eavesdroppers. But I found him a well-informed, interesting and amusing person.

Mohammed Ishaq had an unpretentious office on the upper floor of an old building just off the main bazaar. Below, on the ground floor, were spacious store-rooms, and these in turn opened into an old serai, so that merchandise arriving by caravan from the Persian Gulf or from Bombay could be off-loaded directly at his back door. The store-rooms themselves were generally piled high with bales of goods and, as often as not, there would be more bales lying outside on a verandah, which ran down the two sides of the serai.

One evening Mohammed Ishaq invited me to his home for a meal. I picked him up at his office, and we drove through the outskirts of the town and stopped in a narrow side road flanked by high bare mud walls. It was already dusk and a dejected-looking street lamp threw a fitful arc of yellow light over a big solid wooden door which had once been painted green.

'Not much to look at from the outside,' said my host, as he knocked on the door and called. There was the rattle of a bolt and of a wooden bar being pulled back and the door creaked open. An old gentleman in a long blue coat and round felt hat greeted us as we stepped inside. Then he carefully bolted and barred the door again.

Mohammed Ishaq stepped to the wall, pulled a switch, and a couple of floodlights suspended in the branches of a pomegranate tree lit up a charmingly landscaped garden, complete with a blue-tiled water channel and lily pond. A fair-sized terrace led into the house and, from the quality of the rugs on the floor and the old Persian miniatures on the walls, the owner was a person of good taste and the means to indulge it.

'Yes, it's not a bad specimen,' Mohammed Ishaq said modestly, as I stooped to admire a particularly fine Tekke rug. 'Sit down, and make yourself at home.' He motioned me to a low divan, piled with wool-stuffed saddlebags. 'My wife will be here in a moment.'

I sank into the soft yielding depths of the divan until my posterior was only a couple of inches from the floor, and wondered what further surprises might be in store. My mind conjured up visions of a slim veiled *houri* with gazelle-like eyes, baggy harem trousers and Arabian Nights slippers. Or, a much more likely picture, I imagined some portly bundle of clothing, swathed in black from tip to toe.

The next moment I was struggling clumsily to my feet, for I was in the Presence. She was neither *houri* nor black *chador*-ed matron, but a handsome, dark-eyed woman, many years younger than her husband. She had a graceful figure and a pleasant and vivacious manner. Her curly black hair was cut in a bob, which emphasised the fine curve of her neck and enhanced her youthful appearance.

She wore an orange-coloured silk blouse of western design, open at the throat, and girdled at her waist with a narrow belt of gilded leather. The only oriental items of her dress were her baggy trousers of dark-blue silk. Her feet were clad in dainty golden leather sandals which looked as though they had come direct from Fifth Avenue or Rue de la Paix, and she had pink lacquered toenails. Her jewellery consisted of a pair of jade pendant earrings with a necklace to match and a plain gold wedding ring.

Mohammed Ishaq presented me to his wife, who spoke only Persian and a little French. She asked how I liked Tehran, and we discussed trivialities until a servant announced that the meal was served.

This, like the host and hostess, was a blend of Orient and Occident. The food was typically Persian, the main dish being a very rich *pilau*, not eaten with the fingers, but with spoon and fork. We were also served a claret and with the coffee an excellent French cognac.

We conversed throughout the meal in Persian, out of deference to Madame, but when she later excused herself and gracefully withdrew, Mohammed Ishaq seated himself beside me on the divan, and the conversation, now in English, became less formal.

We started with the subject of wine, because I had expressed some surprise that as a Moslem, my host had shown no reticence in drinking alcohol. On the contrary he had now poured out a second generous portion of cognac, and was cuddling his oversize glass and sniffing the bouquet with all the relish of a connoisseur.

'Wine,' he said, 'is fine in its proper place. It rounds off a good meal, and makes a poor one palatable, but for me give me a good cognac every time. After all, if we are to break the rules and imbibe that which is forbidden, then let's at least get what you call a real kick out of it. Otherwise, what's the good!'

From wine the conversation turned to women and, warmed by the inner glow of the liquor and the atmosphere of intimacy, my host began to let himself go in a happy reminiscent vein.

He clearly considered himself a connoisseur of women and particularly of Iranian women. I suggested that he must have had many interesting adventures, and he cocked a quizzical eye at me over his brandy glass. 'Adventures? Yes, and misadventures, too. Cigarette?'

I shook my head. 'It would spoil the brandy.'

'I know,' he said, 'but I can't help it.' He lit another cigarette.

'One thing you learn when you've lived out here a while is to be damn careful having any relations with the women. I mean, of course, the native women. Believe me, it can be downright dangerous.' He puffed thoughtfully, and paused to watch the tendril of smoke curl slowly upwards.

'That's true of more places than Iran,' I said, and waited for him to continue.

'That may be so, but I'm talking about this country, and take it from me there's still a great deal of religious fanaticism in Iran. As a visitor you may not be conscious of it, but it is there, lurking just below the surface. And there are plenty of religious fanatics only too ready to seize any excuse for making trouble. And on the subject of their own Moslem women, they are particularly sensitive. And so for me especially it was extremely risky having any dealings with a native woman.'

'But why especially for you?' I asked.

'My friend, I ought to explain. For any ordinary Moslem there would be little danger, unless of course he was unlucky and happened to run into the woman's husband. But you see in those days I was not a Moslem, I was a *feringhi*, and what was worse I was a Jew.'

'But would that make much difference?'

'Well, for any *feringhi* caught having an affair with a Persian woman it would mean a stiff fine and a term of imprisonment, and for a Jew they would make the terms even more severe. But for the woman of course it would be much worse. For the woman the usual punishment was death. In the old days they used to drop them from a high building. Later they either threw them into a well, or if there was no well handy, they took them out and stoned them to death.'

'D'you mean it was the law of the country?'

'It was the law of the Mullahs, and whether it was written in the law books or not it frequently used to happen in practice, and probably still does.'

'Seems very unfair on the woman,' I said.

My host grunted. 'Yes, it was tough on the woman.' He

took a deep pull at his cigarette, then exhaled slowly and looked directly at me through the smoke.

'Listen, and I'll tell you what happened with me. Of course, it was quite a number of years ago, and I was younger then and more impulsive.

'I was away down in the country, a good distance from here. I had gone with my appraiser to examine some skins, and we were on our way back. We were driving along a bumpy side road that really was not a road at all. It was getting towards evening, and we noticed a small crowd of villagers some little distance ahead to the right of the road. I saw what looked like a scuffle going on, and there was some shouting.

'As we came nearer, we could hear a woman screaming, and we pulled up to see what it was all about. A villager standing near the road said it was only a family squabble, that a woman had been having an affair and someone had sneaked to her husband about it. Now they were taking the woman out to punish her.'

Mohammed inhaled deeply and blew out a jet of smoke from the corner of his mouth.

'By this time we were quite close and could see what was going on. A man—I supposed he was the husband—was pulling and dragging the wretched woman, and every now and then was hitting her with his fists. Once she stumbled and fell, and the crowd was following close on their heels. Some of them, I could see, were picking up stones as they walked along.

'We were only about thirty paces away by the side of the road and I had halted the car. I didn't know what to do, or whether to do anything, but I opened the door and half got out.

'I think I shouted to the man to wait a bit, or something like that. Anyway, as soon as the woman saw us, she wrenched herself free and dashed straight towards us. Before I could move, she clutched me with both arms and implored me to save her. She had left most of her *chador* in the man's hands, and her face and arms were bare. I was surprised to see that she was quite young and very good-looking.'

Mohammed Ishaq put down his cigarette and picked up his glass. He sipped the brandy slowly and deliberately.

'It was one of those moments,' he went on, 'when one either acts quickly or one does nothing. Had I stopped to think, it might have been wiser not to have interfered, but it would have been death for the woman. There was no doubt about that; those villagers were really out for her blood.

'So without thinking what I was doing, I pulled the girl into the car. "Quick," I said to my companion, "let's get out of here."

'Fortunately Fazal, my appraiser, had his wits about him and we got going immediately. Luckily too I had a bag of krans on the seat of the car. I always carry a quantity of silver when we go into the villages, in case we decide to buy any hides or other produce. I pulled out a handful of the coins and as we moved off I flung them down at the husband's feet, and shouted, "There, take that for her."

'For a moment the silly fool just stood there gaping, but the others ran forward and began frantically to pick up the money. This was too much for the husband and he also hurried to snatch up what he could.

'It was already getting dark, and I hoped that nobody would have noticed the number on the car. We drove for several *farsakhs* along the side road, and then took a short-cut across a field onto the main road to Tehran. We reached the outskirts and Fazal, who was married, stopped at his house and brought out a fresh *chador* for the girl. At that time I was still living in an old house on the other side of the town, so I left the car with Fazal and we, the girl and I, walked home by the side roads without anybody seeing us.'

Mohammed Ishaq reached out for the decanter and replenished our glasses.

I sensed that there was more to come, so settled myself back on the divan again and watched my host.

'Well, Shireen—that was her name—stayed on and lived with me. It was no problem because I was not married and there was no other woman around except the old wife of the cook, who lived on the premises. The house was in a quiet alleyway and had a garden, not as big as this one of course, but with high walls all round it.'

Mohammed Ishaq sniffed his brandy approvingly. 'Shireen was a fine girl. She took charge of the household and made a wonderful mistress. I bought European clothes for her and taught her to speak French, but for a long time I never dared let her go outside the street door. Later, she used to go down into the bazaar, but always in a *chador* and never alone. The old cook's wife always accompanied her. So we lived together very happily for two years and I never felt I wanted any other woman.

'I even thought of marrying Shireen so that I could take her travelling with me, but there was always the religious difficulty, because as I mentioned I was nominally at any rate of the Jewish faith.' He reached out and passed me the cigarettes. I shook my head so he lit one for himself, inhaled deeply and blew the smoke out slowly through his nostrils.

'Yes, we were very happy, in fact so happy that I sometimes wondered if it could possibly last. And then, one day, the storm burst over us.

'It was towards evening, and we were just sitting down to eat, when we heard shouting outside, and people started banging on the big street door.

'Ali, this same servant I have here, came running in with a scared look on his face and what he told me was really alarming. Somebody had been talking in the bazaar. It could only have been one of the gardeners whom I had recently dismissed for thieving. The story had got around that I, a *feringhi* and a Jew, was keeping a Moslem woman in my house as my mistress. The thing must have been carefully worked up, because there was a real mob outside the house and worse still it was headed by a Mullah. Things certainly looked bad.' Mohammed Ishaq took a long sip of brandy.

'I was afraid to open the street door,' he went on, 'and I tried to pacify them, but it was no good. They began throwing stones over the wall and hammered at the door, threatening to break it down. They were demanding that I hand over the woman and they were going to stone her to death there and then.'

'The hell of a situation,' I said.

'You're right,' he said, 'it was a hellish situation. I was scared so badly, that I didn't seem able to think clearly. One thing was certain; the mob were out for blood, the girl's blood in any case, and probably mine as well.

'It was impossible to reach the police and in any case they wouldn't have been able to do much. The more I argued with the crowd, the angrier they became. The banging on the door became louder; they were preparing to break their way in. They wouldn't listen to me, so I asked Ali to treat with them. Finally he talked them into agreeing that the Mullah should be allowed inside to discuss matters.

'Fortunately the Mullah seemed to be older and more sensible than the rest. I gave him a seat and spoke to him with great respect.

'At first I tried to persuade him that the whole thing was a mistake, and I swore that Shireen was not a Moslem. I even had her come and show herself wearing a European frock and speaking French, but apparently the Mullah had heard a good deal of the story—it could only have been that pig of a gardener who had spread it—and he said quite firmly that things had gone too far now to hush the matter up. The crowd had appealed to him as Mullah, and either I would have to settle with him, or the mob would take things into their own hands. If they did this, he warned me, Shireen's would not be the only blood they would spill.'

'Didn't you try to buy him off?' I asked.

'Of course, that was naturally the first thing I thought of,' he smiled indulgently, as though my question were rather childish, 'but it was no use. As the Mullah himself said, things had gone too far for that. No, the girl would have to be handed over, or else—the Mullah had an idea—there might be just one other way out, and that was for me to publicly abjure my own faith and embrace Islam, then formally marry the girl under Moslem law.' Mohammed Ishaq paused dramatically.

'And what did you do?'

'What could I do? What would you have done in my place? I had no choice. I embraced Islam,' he said quite simply, 'and I declared Shireen to be my lawful wife. The Mullah pronounced the necessary formula, and I slipped him something quite substantial with which to seal the contract. In addition I gave him sufficient to buy a fat-tailed sheep to feed the mob.

'He explained things to the crowd in his own manner. They must have been disappointed at being cheated of their sport, but he told them about the sheep and they gradually dispersed with a lot of muttering, and that was the last I heard about it.'

'You were certainly well out of it,' I said, 'but was that really the end of the trouble?'

'Of course the story got around and people talked, but that was a long time ago and finally it was forgotten. I dropped my original names and became Mohammed Ishaq. None of my family were out here in Iran and in any case I didn't care what they might have thought. Later, we moved to this present house and we've lived here happily ever since.'

'So that is Shireen who . . .'

'Yes,' he smiled, 'that is Shireen . . . I have never regretted it,' he said simply, as his hand reached out for the decanter.

Finally came my last day in Tehran. Abdul completed loading up Zobeida with the baggage and fresh supplies of petrol, lubricant and water, while I regretfully took leave of my host and his cheerful colleagues at the Legation. It had been a pleasant ten days, and the time had passed all too rapidly. In particular I had enjoyed the trips to Ray and Shimran, and picnics at the foot of Demavend. They provided a welcome contrast to my prowls with Abdul in the semi-darkness of the bazaars, and the hours spent drinking tea with local merchants, or seated on a bale of merchandise and chatting with Mohammed Ishaq.

It was the people I met in Tehran who pleased and interested me, rather than the city itself. There is none more charming than a really cultured Irani, and I derived much pleasure from meeting them socially and sharing in their conversation.

With the smaller merchants and the shopkeepers of the bazaar I had less in common, yet I had a lot of fun arguing and bargaining with them. But I had finished my work in Tehran, and there was nothing to justify a longer stay. It was time to take to the road again, with Qum and Isfahan my next objective.

Chapter 11

QUM

Skirting the capital, a ring of outlying hamlets form miniature oases with their surrounding patches of cultivation. Soon they are left behind, and the road leads out into the great expanse of sun-dried khaki landscape and continues into the dim distance ahead. Khaki is a Persian word, meaning of the earth (*khak*), earthy, and it is the predominant natural colour of the great central plateau and also of much of the rest of the country. Not only the surface of the terrain is khaki, but the river-beds and the eroded slopes of the lower ranges are the same dull colour. So are the squat, windowless dwellings of the villages, with their surrounding walls, and so too are the caravanserais and the bridges.

With such a parched and uninspiring background, the smallest patch of vegetation comes as a pleasing contrast to the eye. One welcomes the sight of an occasional village, where the drabness and squalor of the buildings are more than compensated for by a surrounding belt of restful green cultivation, a cluster of poplars, willows and mulberry trees, or in spring, a brilliant splash of pink and white fruit blossom.

But there is a silent dignity about the bare, featureless countryside and at certain times, especially in the early morning and late afternoon, the slanting rays of the sun produce surprising effects of light and shadow. The dull khaki groundwork appears a richer yellow-ochre, and its sameness is broken and splashed with lavender-tinted strips and patches, as every stone or clod or shrub lends its individual shadow to the general scheme. Finally the whole picture is framed by the purple and rose-pink mountain ranges rising far off and fringing the sky.

But during the midday period, when the solar rays beat

down vertically and cast least shadow, the colours fade out, the mountains disappear and the horizon closes in. The skyline is obscured in a shimmering haze and there is nothing to break the deadly monotony.

To relieve this tedium, the Iranian roads provide special distractions of their own. One of these, the concealed *joob*, has already been mentioned, but a few more comments may be permitted. For it is impossible not to feel a sneaking admiration for the beaver-like diligence of the peasant who finds the main highway lying directly between his source of water and the land he wants to irrigate. With the simple tool at his disposal, a heart-shaped shovel at the end of a long haft, he cannot tunnel underneath the road, so he is forced to cut across it. The solution is a *joob*. So he gets to work, and after labouring most of the night the result is a perfectly satisfactory channel, with the sides so cleanly and neatly cut that the smallest donkey can take it in his stride.

Such *joobs* presented no obstruction to traffic and nobody had cause for complaint until the advent of motor transport. Then the best-made *joobs* became dangerous booby-traps, and the digger of *joobs* a public menace.

But an even more exasperating hazard, though less dangerous, is the cast-off donkey shoes. I mention donkey shoes specifically, because they seem to be more numerous than mule shoes, though in potential for mischief, there is nothing to choose between them. Horseshoes do not come into question because there are relatively so few.

In the course of centuries, untold generations of baggage animals have left jagged fragments of iron lying in profusion along the country's highways. Concealed beneath a thin coating of pulverous Iranian *khak*, like a modern military minefield, they lie in readiness for unsuspecting wheeled transport to pass that way.

Despite the mass of superstition with which the country is ridden, nobody seems to have spread the belief that finding a donkey shoe brings good luck, and it is left to the motorist to discover them in his tyres.

One soon learns to dread that sudden cobra-like hiss and

bumping drag. One brakes and gets down and there is the little brute—three or more inches of jagged iron—protruding from the flattened tyre. And for the umpteenth time, as one flings the noxious fragment across the open waste, one curses and burns the father of the inventor of all iron shoes.

As we progressed along the highway we met with little traffic, but every few miles or so a distant blur on the road ahead, distorted by mirage, would resolve itself into a string of mules or donkeys, laden with bales of produce or merchandise. There would be a brief jingling of bells and a passing glimpse of a tanned, lean-faced muleteer. One shouted a *Salaam Aleikum*, heard the faint receding answer, and the road ahead was empty again.

At one point we sighted a couple of blurred objects away in front of us, and some little distance off the road. As we got nearer they turned out to be a man and a donkey. The man was elderly, with a bright-red henna-dyed beard, and he was squatting on a hummock of rock, while his ass was tethered a few paces to one side. The whole terrain round about was a flat outcrop of rock. It seemed a strange and remote place for anybody to be sitting and something in the man's behaviour aroused my curiosity.

As we drew nearer he got quickly to his feet, then stooped to pick up a piece of black drapery which lay beside him, and strode hastily to a spot several metres away. There he stood and faced us, holding the drape like a screen in front of him.

Still curious, I stopped the car and Abdul and I got out.

As we approached the old man and greeted him, he did not reply but became visibly agitated. Then as we came up to him he abruptly turned his back on us and, muttering something which I could not make out, stooped down again and made as if to spread the drape on the ground. At that moment the breeze caught the black cloth and it billowed out. Then I grasped the cause of the excitement.

There was a rectangular cavity cut into the rock like a four-sided well, about five feet deep, and the old man was trying to cover this. Glancing to see what he was trying to conceal, I saw the head, and bare arms and shoulders of a young woman. For a moment I thought we had come upon a murder, and visions of faithless wives in wells flashed through my mind. Then the girl looked up and I saw that her face and hair were dripping wet. The next moment the old man succeeded in spreading the drape—it was the girl's *chador*—over the hole, and he faced us in angry protest. We apologised and turned away. The lady was only having a bath.

Nearby, cut into the same table of rock, were several similar holes, each containing a couple or more feet of water. We spent a few minutes examining them. The water was pleasantly warm and gave off a strong sulphurous smell.

Meanwhile the man, who was old enough to be the girl's grandfather, but was evidently her husband, had got her out of the pit and enveloped her safely in her *chador*. When he had loaded her onto the donkey, we went up and talked with him. He spoke some strange dialect which even Abdul could scarcely understand. He explained that this particular locality was known as Garm-Ab, 'warm-waters', that the baths were of great antiquity and famous for their medicinal qualities.

As we climbed back into the car, we exchanged the usual farewell greeting, '*Khuda hafiz*! God protect you!' and Abdul added, 'and Allah grant thy desire!'

'Why did you say that?' I asked.

'He badly wants a son.'

'I didn't hear him say that.'

'*Nakhair*, Agha. He didn't say so, but who would travel all that distance merely to give his wife a bath in stinking water? He told us that the water is famous for its *qudrat*, its power-giving qualities.'

'Then surely grandpa should have had the bath,' I said.

'What petition may I make,' Abdul shrugged. 'Perhaps he had one before we came along.'

For anyone interested in natural history, the wildlife in these upland tracts is disappointingly scarce and the song of a bird is rarely heard. Hawks and foxes and minor predators scour the sunbaked wastes and compete with each other for whatever living sustenance they can find. Occasionally a few gazelle go scampering away into the distance, and it is surprising how they seem to thrive in the most arid and barren places. Some years ago I was astonished to find gazelle on some of the smaller uninhabited and to all appearances completely sterile and waterless islands in the Persian Gulf. How they got there in the first place and how they managed to survive remained a mystery.

A question which has long interested me is whether the lion and the *gur*, the wild ass, are still extant in Iran, or whether as is generally believed they are already extinct.

On my way through the country I surprised a lot of people by posing this question. It was clearly useless asking any city-bred persons; they would only have gaped in wonderment and regarded me as mentally afflicted. *Charvadars*, the muleteers and caravan folk, who have spent their whole lives on the road, would be the best informed on such matters, and it was mainly from them that I tried to get the information. Several of the older men declared they remembered having seen wild asses a long time ago. In those days, they said, there were plenty of *gur* living like gazelle in the wide open spaces, but they had not seen any for very many years. They were all very hazy about details and I could not pin them down to any specific localities.

On the subject of lions, I did meet a man who claimed to have seen one. He was a Bakhtiari tribesman, and he said he had seen the animal some five or six years previously in hilly country about twenty-five kilometres from Dizful. He had been riding a pony at the time. His mount had smelt the lion and had shied and tried to bolt before he himself saw it. As he had no weapon he did not wait to observe the animal, but let the pony have its head and galloped away.

Sir Percy Sykes once told me that he had seen the dead body of a lion floating down the Karun river when it was in flood. But a more recent sighting was reported by two American engineers working on road construction, also not far from Dizful. Early one morning they saw a lion and lioness drinking from a pool in a river-bed. They hurried back to camp to get a rifle, but when they returned the lions had disappeared.

So far as I am aware, no sightings of lion in Iranian territory have been reported since then, but I think it would be premature, even now, to say that the Iranian lion is finally extinct. On the other hand, if any of them have survived, they would only be found in the more remote areas of south-western Iran. There is no doubt that at one time lions roamed widely and in considerable numbers across the Syrian desert and Mesopotamia and thence up onto the Iranian plateau. From there they would naturally find their way through the wild country of Beluchistan into Kathiawar and the Scind desert. This would explain the presence, even today, of lions in the Gir jungles of Kathiawar, the only area in Asia where *Felis leo* is still definitely known to exist in his original wild state, though now limited in number and strictly preserved. There seems no doubt that the Gir lions are an offshoot of the Iranian lion, which in turn is the same species as the African, though without such a fine mane.

To many travellers in the interior of Iran the most pleasing and also the most characteristic feature of the countryside is the *chae-khaneh*, the wayside tea-houses, scattered at irregular intervals along the main highways.

The Iranian tea-house is an institution as ancient as the caravanserai, for ever since human beings began travelling about, whether on foot or on animal-back, there has been the need for food and shelter. Through many centuries the two institutions were equally vital to the traveller, but since the development of motor transport the caravanserais, to a great extent, have lost their *raison d'être*, and are falling more and more into disuse and decay. Today few of the old country serais are still in use, except where, especially in the larger cities, they have been adapted to modern conditions and serve as garages, parking places and storage units. But for many of the tea-houses, just as with the old coaching inns in western Europe, the advent of the motor car has meant renewed vitality and prosperity.

In the larger *chae-khaneh's*, particularly those near the bigger cities, the proprietor will probably be too busy to give individual attention to his customer, and a *ghulam*—literally a slave, but actually a servant, and frequently quite a young urchin—will come and take one's order, and then serve one with a glass of steaming hot tea poised on a saucer.

Often a second *ghulam* tends the samovar, replenishing the water as it is drawn off, and keeping the little china teapot filled with stock-solution. This is just about normal strength by western standards, but little more than one teaspoonful of the brew would be poured into the glass, which is then filled up with boiling water from the samovar.

Then a third *ghulam* will be charged with the sole duty of serving the customers with *qalians*, or water-pipes. In the better-class tea-houses the duty of servicing the water-pipes is carried out by one particular *ghulam*, known as the *Qalianji*, or Master of the Pipes. He is in sole charge of the stocks of tobacco, and he cleans and fills and lights the pipes in readiness for the customers.

The *qalian* consists of three parts—the cup or container, the water-bowl, preferably made of glass though often of earthenware, and the stem or tube, with its mouth-piece. The tobacco is usually kept stored in stone or earthenware jars in the rear part of the building and the dried leaves are broken and reduced to the desired consistency, ready for use. The *Qalianji* places a measured quantity of this into the cup, which he then plugs into the bowl of the *qalian*, already half-filled with water.

Next, the *Qalianji* picks out with a pair of tongs a small piece of glowing charcoal from the brazier and places it on top of the tobacco in the cup. In some cases a piece of smouldering cow- or camel-dung is either substituted for or placed with the charcoal. Some *qalian*-smokers prefer the dung to the charcoal, as being less injurious to the lungs and more agreeable to the palate. *Chacun à son goût*!

Occasionally, as a fanciful touch, a few drops of perfume may be added to the water to give it a tone, and in the better-class tea-houses some attempt is made to wash the mouthpieces of the pipes after each customer. In actual practice, the *ghulam* usually dips them quickly into a clay jar of water, shakes them out, and leaves the customer to deal with the germs.

Some of the more fastidious patrons carry their own amber or ivory mouth-piece with them, just as they carry their own amber rosaries. There is no great art in smoking a *qalian*, or *narghileh*, as it is alternatively called in Iran, or *chilm* in Afghanistan, or *hookah* (or hubble-bubble, colloquially) in India. It is mainly a question of lung power. One inhales with a deep breath and fills the lungs to bursting point with smoke of varying degrees of pungency, holds it as long as possible and then exhales in one continuous action.

In theory at least the smoke is filtered as it passes through the water, and the smoker gets the added pleasure of seeing the bubbles in the bowl, and perhaps finds something soporific in the sound of them, but it is doubtful if the water really eliminates all the noxious charcoal fumes which have mingled with those from the tobacco. Judging by the raucous coughing and throat-clearing that goes on in any *chae-khaneh*, *qalian*-smoking must be an irritating form of pleasure.

It was already after midday when we caught the distant glint of sunlight on a golden dome, and knew we were approaching Qum.

I had heard and read so much about the sanctity of this holy city, that I was most disappointed by the awful drabness of the place. Apart from the great mosque with the shrine, on which the city's fame is based, there is nothing to distinguish Qum from any other medium-sized Iranian township, unless it is the unusually large number of caravanserais for the convenience of pilgrims and for the bodies of their dead relatives brought to the holy city for interment.

There is no recorded history of Qum prior to the Moslem invasion, and this has led to the belief by some scholars that it was the original Arab invaders who actually founded the city. Against this theory is the fact that a tenth-century Arab historian named El Baladhuri records that the Arabs captured an already existing town of Qum in 23 AH (AD 644), while other early records mention the existence of an ancient Iranian fortress on the site at the time of the first Islamic invasion.

What is well established is that during the early years of the Moslem occupation, numbers of Shiah Moslems fleeing from their Arab homeland because of Sunni persecution took refuge in Qum, which gradually became a recognised centre of the Shiah sect. Friction ensued between the Shiah inhabitants and the Sunni governors, and this in turn gradually built up into open antagonism which came to a head during the ninth century, when for long periods the Shiah population refused to pay taxes to their Sunni rulers. As a result, the Caliph Harun-ar-Rashid decided to take strong measures against them in AD 800. The people of Qum were temporarily subdued, but a few years later they renewed their refusal to pay taxes, whereupon Baghdad again despatched a punitive force, this time killing a considerable number of the recalcitrant townspeople, while imposing heavy penalties upon the survivors. Even this drastic action did not end the hostility of the people of Qum towards the Abbasid Caliphs, which continued into the tenth century, and resulted in yet a third punitive expedition.

In AD 1221 came the terrible Mongol invasion. The greater part of the population was slaughtered and the city ravaged and destroyed. Slowly Qum recovered and during the following century and a half no further disaster occurred. Then Tamerlane (Timur) and his hordes appeared upon the scene. They captured the town only after a long and bitter resistance, for which once again the population paid heavily in blood, and their homes were devastated.

The veneration which Qum enjoys dates back to the year AD 816 in which Fatima, the sister of the Imam 'Ali al-Riza at Meshed, while travelling on a visit to her brother, was taken ill and brought to Qum, where she subsequently died and was buried. For nearly eight centuries the tomb of Fatima attracted no attention. It was only in the reign of Shah Abbas the Great (AD 1587–1629) that Qum emerged from its obscurity and became a famous place of pilgrimage. The Shah was desirous of encouraging his subjects to spend their money on pilgrimages to shrines within his own realm, rather than, as very large numbers were wont to do, in visiting the Shiah holy places at Kerbela in Mesopotamia. Instead, he urged them to visit the already greatly revered shrine of the Imam Riza at Meshed, and that of the Imam's sister at Qum.

To this end he had a fine shrine erected over Fatima's tomb, and appealed to all devout subjects to patronise these two holy cities. The Shah's efforts bore fruit. Qum soon became the goal of several thousands of devout worshippers every year, as well as the second most sacred city in the whole of Iran. Later in the seventeenth century, Shah Safi, Shah Abbas II and Shah Suleiman were each buried at Qum, and thus set the pattern for prominent Shiah notables and wealthy citizens to be buried within the precincts of the holy city. Indeed, today, Iranians of all classes regard burial at Qum as something eminently desirable.

The great golden dome and minarets of the Mosque and Shrine of Fatima al-Ma'suma can be seen by even an unbeliever from a respectable distance, but it is advisable not to loiter in the vicinity, especially with a camera. I was unfortunate in that while I was there the light was too poor for a successful photograph.

Even today Qum still retains the reputation of being the centre of much religious bigotry, and it was Mohamed Ishaq in Tehran who told me that the new Shah, Reza Pahlavi, would have to be very careful in his avowed intention to introduce reforms along the lines of those formulated by Mustafa Kemal in Turkey, and most particularly in regard to that extremely delicate question, the emancipation of women. Otherwise, he would inevitably incur the hostility of the fanatical elements in Qum, who were capable of creating very serious trouble throughout the country. In times of internal unrest, the holy city would almost certainly be a dangerous trouble spot.

I had now seen all that could be seen of the Mosque of

Fatima, and with a bitter wind blowing strongly from the north and sky heavily overcast, I decided not to linger in such unfriendly surroundings, and was glad to get into the car and start off again, southbound for Isfahan.

Chapter 12

ISFAHAN

Isfahan is unlike the majority of cities in Iran. Instead of acres of drab mud walls, squat buildings and vistas of dilapidation and ruin, relieved in some few instances by a stream with a cluster of willow or poplar trees, the approaches to this old Safavid capital lead kilometre after kilometre through a green belt of market gardens and fruit orchards. The cultivation is so dense and so extensive that the first impression from a distance is of a tract of woodland without the vestige of a town.

It is only as one approaches nearer that one perceives domes and minarets rising above the fruit trees. Entering the cultivated area the road leads past a succession of humble dwellings, the homes of the cultivators, with an occasional domed shrine and a number of solidly built round towers protruding from the crops and orchards. These resemble somewhat the old Palmyrene burial towers, only they are not tombs but pigeon houses. Many of them date back to Safavid times, some even earlier, when the pigeons were protected and encouraged for their guano.

One supposes that the logicians of the period calculated that the fertilising value of the guano more than offset the heavy toll the pigeons must have taken from the crops. There were many of these towers but I saw few pigeons. Perhaps they were away foraging farther afield, or possibly the present-day Isfahani had been converted to the use of artificial manures, and had ceased to encourage the birds. I suggested that the townspeople might have eaten them.

'Oh no, Agha, no!' Abdul sounded shocked. 'No true follower of Ali would kill a pigeon. They are treated with great respect, because they never tire of repeating *Ya-hu* out of reverence for the Prophet, "on whom be peace".'

Away on the side, rising high above the level of cultivation, is a range of hills whose contours suggest a volcanic origin. On its summit an old ruined structure stands out sharply against the skyline. Abdul, reacting to the less frigid temperature of the valley, un-muffled himself from the folds of his filthy old kaftan and began to take an interest in his surroundings again. He pointed to the ruin on the hill-top and explained that it had once been an *atash-gah* or fire-temple of the *atash-prastan*, the fire-worshipping Zoroastrians, and near it, he said was a very deep well, going down right into the heart of the earth. Nobody knew who had dug the well, perhaps the fire-worshippers, but it was very ancient. It was not in use today. There was no cultivation up there but the Moslems had found a practical use for it. They dropped all their faithless wives into it!

I stayed a week in Isfahan, enjoying the kind hospitality of the bank manager. He was most helpful in giving me introductions to prominent members of the business community, but as in the other towns I had visited I found that the local people could tell me little that I had not already learned from my host.

The morning following my arrival I got up at daybreak and strolled along the broad tree-lined avenue called the Chahar Bagh. There was already a touch of spring in the air, and the chenars and poplars were just bursting into bud. I consider the chenar (the Oriental Plane Tree) to be one of the most beautiful and majestic of all deciduous trees. There is beauty in its bulky mottled trunk, as well as in its graceful branch system, and in the delicate tracery of its foliage. There are a few fine specimens scattered about the surroundings of Isfahan, and some of them might well have been planted in the time of the great Shah Abbas, though are hardly to be compared with their counterparts in the Chenar Bagh and Shalimar gardens of Srinagar in Kashmir. Unfortunately most of those inside the town have been ruined by excessive lopping, maltreatment, or neglect.

From the Chahar Bagh I came out into the wide open space of the Meidan and paused involuntarily to contemplate a scene of unforgettable beauty, as the first rays of dawn turned domes and minarets into a glowing spendour of turquoise, jade and amber. At the southern end of the huge Meidan, the blue dome and multi-coloured minarets and portal of the Masjid-i-Shah, the Royal Mosque, glittered in the early sunlight. On the east side, facing the palace known as the Ali Qapu, or Lofty Gateway, the hemispherical dome of a second seventeenth-century mosque, the Masjid-i-Sheikh Lutfullah, the father-in-law of Shah Abbas I, with its many-hued floral pattern and lofty portal, encased likewise in shining variegated tilework, presented a riot of colour with yellow ochre predominant, recalling the vivid hues of a Kirmani carpet.

A fine morning haze served to tone down the scene, producing a soft luminous radiance that lent enchantment, and more than compensated for the many hundreds of kilometres of drab landscape I had crossed to reach here.

There were as yet few people moving about. A couple of early risers were cantering their frisky Arab-type ponies over the spacious surface of the Meidan. With a jingling of bells, a string of four mules paced briskly past me. The leading animal wore a good luck talisman of bright blue beads round his neck. Three mules were laden with baskets of fresh vegetables, the fourth carried his master seated astride his rear haunches. They were doubtless heading for the bazaars, whose main entrance, a large archway, was at the other end of the Meidan. In front of the entrance stood two stone columns, original goalposts for the polo matches which formerly used to be played here by the Shah and his nobles. These games must have been exciting to watch for we are told that the numbers of the players, as well as the rules of the game, varied considerably.

An air of restful quiet pervaded the entire Meidan, in the absence of the bustle and clamour and the harsh impact of the modern world. There were no motor-cars, not even a bicycle, to recall the mechanical age. Transport was by horse, mule, or donkey, as it had been for centuries. With few exceptions, even the dress of the common people showed little change. Reza Shah had indeed introduced by edict that monstrosity, the Pahlavi cap, but most of the working- and peasant-class people I saw in the streets of Isfahan still wore the picturesque dome-shaped felt, rather like a brimless London bowler. Many of the educated classes wore the circular *karakul* or sheepskin hat, or a tightly tied white turban and for dress, a loosely flowing kaftan. It was this pleasing old-world atmosphere which distinguished Isfahan from any other town I had so far seen in Iran. Almost all of them, with the exception of Tehran, had a long history behind them, and most of them boasted at least a few ancient ruins to record it. But however striking these may have been, they were nothing more than individual relics and did not of themselves create an atmosphere.

It was Shah Abbas the Great who was the creator of Isfahan's many-coloured splendour. We had seen evidence of his high architectural standards in the bridges and caravanserais encountered as we travelled across the country, but it was in the planning and conversion of Isfahan into the imperial capital that the Shah's love of design and colour were given a free hand. He planned on a royal scale; the very size of the Meidan bears testimony to this, for it served as a parade ground for his troops as well as for polo and other outdoor pursuits. For the lay-out of the splendid main avenue, the Shah allocated the land from four separate vineyards or orchards, hence the name Chahar Bagh, or Four Gardens. He also constructed a fine bridge across the river, comprising an upper and a lower row of arches and named it after one of his generals, Allahverdi Khan. It is also popularly known as the Pul-i-Chahar Bagh.

About one kilometre to the south-east is another fine old bridge, dating from the fifteenth century and reconstructed in its present form in the reign of Shah Abbas II (1642–66). Like its Chahar Bagh companion, it also has an upper and lower row of arches, and the lower row stands on broad projecting platforms of cut stone blocks rising only about one metre above water-level. During the warm weather these platforms attract crowds of townsfolk, who like to sit there and 'eat the air' to the sound of the muddy Zayandeh Rud flowing at their feet.

Back at the Meidan, the light morning mist had lifted and the colouring of the tiled domes became more vivid. I suddenly realised that though time might appear to stand still, my watch continued to go. I must loiter no longer, but go straight back or be late for breakfast.

During the following days I took time off to explore the less central parts of the town, and visit the remaining historic monuments. Most notable of these is the Masjid-i-Jami. This is the oldest of the principal mosques, for it dates back to the late eleventh century and the reign of the Seljuq Sultan Malik Shah. While much less decorative than the later Safavid mosques, with its two separate domes it is considered by experts to be structurally one of the finest surviving specimens of Seljuq architecture.

The Madraseh-ye-Mader-i-Shah, begun in 1706 and completed nine years later, is smaller and later than most of the other historic buildings. It is not a mosque, but a *dar-ul-ulum*, or seat of learning. Non-Moslems are not excluded, and the unbeliever may enter its precincts and admire the exquisite tilework unmolested.

Besides the mosques and the madraseh and a number of tomb-shrines, there are several royal palaces. Of these the two earliest are the Chihil Sutun (late sixteenth century) and Ali Qapu (early seventeenth). Chihil Sutun means Forty Pillars. I did not trouble to count them because 'forty' in Persian is commonly used as a figure of speech to signify 'many', as in the Forty Thieves.

With its pillars and pine trees and spacious verandah reflected in a *hauz* (lake), the Chihil Sutun has the airy appearance of a summer pleasance rather than a palace. The Ali Qapu, on the other hand, is more solid and less attractive.

I was more impressed by the two long bridges, the Pul-i-Allahverdi and Pul-i-Khaju, which span the wide and stony stream-bed of the Zayandeh Rud. The name means Living River, but it is scarcely appropriate since, except in summer when melting mountain snows bring it down in flood, the stream is barely more than a feeble trickle.

The main entrance to the bazaars from the Meidan-i-Shah is in keeping with their original grandeur. Approaching them in bright sunshine from the open Meidan, one is at first conscious only of a lofty decorated archway enveloped in deep shadow. On entering the shade, one's eyes adjust themselves to the gloom, the archway assumes form and colour, and the surroundings take on a soft bluish hue. Blue is everywhere predominant. It gleams in the ubiquitous tilework and in the painted wooden frames of the doorways. The full-length garments favoured by working men are dyed bright indigo, and blue lurks in almost every Irani rug. Even the sky appears a richer blue than in other parts of the country and the very shadows reflect its azure richness.

As one gropes one's way through the soft half-light, pierced here and there by golden shafts of sunlight streaming through apertures in the vaulted roof, one senses a cathedral-like atmosphere, an entrancing air of remoteness from the outer world.

Then one begins to notice the signs of neglect. Many of the lanes of shops are abandoned, and there are large areas of sunlit ruins where the vaulting has fallen in. Piles of crumbling debris foretell the fate already threatening the surviving structures. The loss to Isfahan from a historical point of view if the old bazaars were allowed to disappear completely, would be most regrettable. Together with the mosques, the madraseh and the royal palaces they formed part of the original Safavid capital. However, much of the dilapidated area might be removed without detracting from the appearance of the whole. Indeed, the grandeur of the Great Mosque would be vastly enhanced if the jungle of surrounding buildings could be cleared away.

*

I wished I could have remained longer in Isfahan. Those early morning strolls across the wide Meidan were alone worth staying for. The light effects at dawn were never the same two mornings in succession, and altogether Isfahan remains in my memory as the most attractive of all Iranian cities.

I made a practice of writing up my notes at night, and thus found time to spare for some aimless but pleasurable rambling. Sometimes I strolled around on my own, but I found it more fun to have Abdul with me.

The language was no problem, but city dwellers were less ready to talk to strangers, especially to a *feringhi*, than were the ordinary country-people. Here in Isfahan, while the common folk always seemed ready to stop and chat, the more sophisticated educated classes would respond automatically to your greeting with *W'aleikum salaam*, but would then look at you askance and veer away, as though shunning closer contact with a *kafir* (unbeliever). Yet when Abdul was with me there was no such reticence. He would greet anyone from a dervish to a beggar, and would engage them in conversation into which I too would be drawn.

His strong points were arguing and bargaining. He could haggle both hind legs off even an Isfahani donkey. I had discovered this one day when I was doing a little private dickering over a small tribal prayer-rug. The shopkeeper and I had just about reached a deadlock, when Abdul tugged at my sleeve and drew me away from the shop.

'You want that rug very much, Agha?'

'I'd like it, but . . .'

'How much are you prepared to give?'

I mentioned a sum a little more than half the price I had worked the dealer down to.

'*Kheili khub*, Agha. Very good. You give me the money and go away and leave it to me.'

That evening when I returned to my room the prayer-rug was already there, spread on my bed.

'How did you do it?' I asked. But Abdul only shrugged and

smiled mysteriously. 'I know these people, Agha,' was all he would say.

Among local business people in Isfahan I had been given an introduction to an Armenian merchant named Tutunjian, and I called on him at his office in the suburb of Julfa, across the river.

I found Mr Tutunjian an agreeable and cultured gentleman who spoke fluent English as well as French. He was *dunya-deedeh*, as they say in Iran of one who has travelled widely and seen the world. He appeared to have varied commercial interests, including the export of carpets and rugs, and his business had taken him to London, Paris and New York.

We discussed the general situation and Mr Tutunjian gave me much useful information. Then he invited me to accompany him to his home to take coffee. It was only a short walk from his office to the house, and my host led me into his comfortably furnished study, and called to a servant to bring coffee and a bottle of wine.

'You may not care for our coffee,' he said, 'that is imported, but we are rather proud of our wine, for we make it ourselves. It is one of the few privileges enjoyed by a Christian minority in a Moslem country.'

I said I had read about the Armenian suburb of Julfa, but felt vague as to its origin.

'Well, there's no great mystery about how it came into being,' Tutunjian said, 'it was founded by Shah Abbas at the time he was building up Isfahan as his imperial capital, but the reasons why he did so are not so clear.'

At this moment the door opened and an Armenian servant came in carrying a tray with a pot of coffee and glasses, and a bottle of red wine. He placed them on a small table with a carved brass top, set a large silver box of cigarettes beside them, and quietly withdrew.

'Let's try the wine first,' said my host, and poured out two glasses.

It was a fruity, full-bodied wine, not as sweet or as smooth as Malaga, and without the quality of a Burgundy, but otherwise quite palatable. I praised its flavour and Tutunjian, evidently pleased, told me to make myself comfortable in an armchair and settled himself in his own. He poured out two cups of coffee, added sugar and placed them conveniently within reach, also the cigarette box.

'You were telling me about the founding of Julfa,' I said, as we lighted our cigarettes.

'Yes. Well, of course you know that this Julfa takes its name from the original Julfa up on the northern border of Azerbaijan. That other Julfa was a very ancient city and at the time of Shah Abbas it was also very prosperous. The inhabitants were mostly Armenians and being Christians were under frequent attack by the Tatars of Azerbaijan. The town was therefore very vulnerable. Shah Abbas was well aware of this, and also of the fact that Julfa was a wealthy city, and a constant temptation to the Tatars to attack it. The Shah decided to remove the temptation by transferring the entire population and resettling them down here, just across the river from his own capital. The new colony was called Julfa after the old city. Then to avoid friction with the Moslem religious elements in Isfahan the Christian Armenians were compelled to live strictly within the limits of their new colony and were forbidden to do business in Isfahan.'

'Is the ban still in force today?' I asked.

'It remained in force for three hundred years, but now under the present regime it has been relaxed, and our merchants and tradespeople are moving freely to the modern commercial quarter on the other side of the river.

'Of course,' Tutunjian went on, 'nobody knows for certain what really motivated Shah Abbas. It's possible that the Shah really wished to avoid friction and involvement with the Tatars when he was so fully occupied with his construction plans down here, but it's also possible that his principal motive was to bring money and trade to his new capital, and he cast around for a quick and ready way of doing so, while using the Tatars as an excuse. What does seem to be well established is that the Armenian citizens of the old Julfa were reluctant to leave their homes in Azerbaijan, but the Shah compelled them to do so by cutting off all their irrigation channels and water supply.'

Although the Iranian crowds were becoming accustomed to *feringhis* wielding cameras, I still found much reluctance on the part of mothers to have their children photographed. I had already a collection of Afghan children's photographs taken in the frontier tribal areas, and others taken among Kurds and Arabs. Some of them I had had difficulty in securing owing to the shyness of the parents, particularly the women, and here I was now meeting with the same difficulty.

One morning, outside a doorway in the Chahar Bagh, I spotted a little girl standing beside a giant Ali Baba jar as tall as herself. She was one of the prettiest children I had so far come across and in that setting she made a perfect picture.

With Abdul close behind me, I was focusing my camera when the child's mother rushed forward, chattering excitedly, and pushed the child angrily aside. Abdul exclaimed '*Ma sha'allah*! what God wills!' and repeated it very clearly. He even offered the woman a couple of krans, but she waved them aside and, still muttering, seized the child by the arm and dragged her away from the doorway.

'*Chashm-i-shur*,' Abdul said laconically and shrugged his shoulders.

'Evil-eye be damned,' I said. 'Didn't you see that great lump of turquoise the kid had strung round her neck? Surely that was big enough to keep off any evil-eye?'

'*Che arz kunam*,' Abdul gave a shrug of helplessness. 'Didn't I say *ma sha'allah* twice, and that should have been strong enough. But what can you do with these women!' He shrugged again. 'Yet you must admit that the child was exceptionally beautiful.'

'That's just why I wanted her picture.'

'And that's just why the woman was so scared. The danger's always greater with the pretty ones.'

'What d'you mean, the danger's always greater? What danger? Did she think I might give her little brat the smallpox?'

'Not that, Agha, but you don't know these women, how frightened they are of the *chashm-i-shur*. Perhaps I should have repeated *ma-sha'allah* a third time; it might have worked.'

'But surely you don't believe all this non . . .' I checked myself, for I could see I was on delicate ground, 'all this evil-eye business?'

'*Che arz kunam*, Agha,' Abdul's eyebrows went up in that irritating manner which I had come to take as meaning 'Why ask these silly questions when you know you won't agree with me anyhow?' He continued, 'Sometimes, without doubt, it is only women's foolishness, but sometimes it could be real. It is difficult to tell.'

'Then you really do believe in the power of the evil-eye?'

'I do not believe that everybody has the power. Allah help us if that were so. But some people do have it and make use of it. Others have it but do not know they have it, and that makes them very dangerous.'

One cannot live long in the East without coming in contact with this superstition, but Abdul evidently had definite ideas about it, so I asked him to explain.

'*Bibineed*, Agha, see here. It is well known that Allah alone can create anything perfect, and it is wicked for any man to try and equal Allah. *Durust ast*? Isn't that so?'

He looked at me and I nodded. '*Durust ast*. Yes, that's correct.'

'If he does so, then surely evil will befall both him and that which he has made.' He paused and I nodded again.

'Therefore no man will ever make, for example, a perfect rug or a perfect archway, for fear of bringing down the wrath of Allah.'

'I know,' I said, 'so he leaves the pattern unfinished, or makes it irregular, or he puts in one stone more on one side of the arch than on the other . . .'

'*Durust*, Agha, and why?'

'You tell me why,' I said.

'Because somebody with the salty-eye might come along and look at it, and if there was no blemish or fault in it, they might admire and praise it, and that would surely bring down misfortune upon both the maker and his work.'

'But how do the mother and child come into this?' I asked.

'For the same reason, Agha. No human child is perfect, and therefore he should not be admired as such. It might be taken as a kind of worship, Agha, and Allah will not tolerate that. For there is but one Allah, who alone is *kamil*, perfect, and to be praised. So if a child is very beautiful, the danger of anyone admiring his beauty is greater than if he were not so beautiful.'

'But may not even the mother admire her own child?'

'She may think her child beautiful, but she would never dare say so in words. She would fear that some other person might say so, and if that person were an unbeliever—a *feringhi*—the danger would be still greater, and that is why she was so frightened and hurried the child away.'

'But why all this *ma sha'allah*, *ma sha'allah* business?'

'That is to keep away the *chashm-i-shur*, the salty-eye, Agha. For ordinary persons one *ma sha'allah* is sufficient. Because there were two of us, I said it twice. But because you are a *feringhi*, I should, perhaps, have said it three times.'

'Abdul,' I said, 'sometimes you amaze me.'

'*Che arz kunam*,' he murmured, as we pursued our walk.

But his explanation rang a bell in my memory. I recalled another case, that of an Afridi woman in the Khyber. The Afridis are extremely fanatical and ridden with superstition. This woman too had a particularly pretty child, and fearing to evoke the evil-eye, she actually named him *Ma-sha'allah* so that anyone speaking to him would themselves first utter the charm that fended off the evil.

Mashallah Khan survived his boyhood, but in the pride of his early manhood he was killed in a frontier skirmish. (Had the charm worn off, or was it not proof against bullets?)

And there was the case of another Pathan, a young Khattak sepoy, again an unusually handsome lad. He belonged to one of those tribal clans who claim descent from the original warriors and colonists of Alexander the Great. He had a classic profile with bobbed hair in the traditional Greek style and large 'gazelle-like' eyes, such as Pathans love to sing about.

His mother feared that those eyes would be her son's undoing, so, for his protection, he had been named Yek-Bin, or One-Eye. Despite some risky amorous adventures in his youth, he survived to join a regiment. As Sepoy Yek-Bin Khan he went unscathed through numerous forays, but eventually came to grief when his patrol was ambushed by a tribal raiding party. In his case too the evil-eye had been foiled, but not the bullet.

Later on the road Abdul told me much more about the *Chashm-i-shur*. In other parts of the country, he said, it was known as the *Chashm-i-zakhm* or 'wounding-eye'. Some people also called it *Chasm-i-tang*, or 'narrow-eye'. The victim who came under its influence was said to be *chashm-zuddeh*, or 'eye-struck'.

The utterance of the Arabic words *ma-sha'allah*, What God wills, is not just a popular belief, Abdul insisted, but is prescribed by the Qoran itself, and therefore should be infallible. However, many people prefer to take no chances, and try to render themselves or the objects of their affection doubly secure by means of a talisman.

This may be anything from a small amulet hung round the neck, or bound round the arm, and containing a text from the Qoran, to a necklace of blue beads.

Iranian beggars, like Iranian bazaars, have much in common with their counterparts all over Asia. They are abject, they are disgustingly dirty, and they beg. But also, like the bazaars which they frequent, they reflect in some degree the character of the country itself.

Taken as a crowd, the beggars of Iran are less offensive than those in many other Asian lands. There is a charming roguishness about them which, in myself at all events, evokes a sympathy I rarely feel for Arab or Indian mendicants. The Iranian beggar may be a bigger humbug, but he has a certain subtlety of manner entirely lacking in the others.

Abdul did not share my feelings and disliked my wasting good *baksheesh*, which he felt might be better spent elsewhere.

'Never give to a beggar, Agha, unless he is a Saiyid and then, of course, one must give.'

'Why must? One's surely not obliged to give alms to a Saiyid beggar?'

'*Beli*, Agha, It is a *farz*, a sacred duty.'

'Why?' I asked. 'Is it because a Saiyid is supposed to be a descendant of the Prophet?'

'Not only that, Agha, but because the Prophet, on Whom be peace, said, "One-fifth of your goods must ye give to the Saiyids".'

'But surely the Prophet never meant all Saiyid descendants throughout the centuries?'

'What He meant is known only to Allah, but that is what He said, and thus it is written. And the Saiyid beggars know it well, and never let one forget it.'

'Are there many Saiyid beggars?'

'Very, very many, Agha, but they do not *beg* for alms, but demand them as a sacred duty.'

'But, apart from beggars, are Saiyids considered holier than other Moslems?'

'They are shown greater respect, Agha, particularly by the womenfolk. If their child is sick, they will take a piece of bread to a Saiyid for him to touch it with his tongue.'

'How on earth can that help?'

'Because, Agha, the spittle of the Prophet has healing powers, and a true Saiyid being a descendant of the Prophet, claims to have the same healing power in his spittle. Of course,' Abdul added with a twinkle in his eye, 'all Saiyids are not true children of the Prophet, and so the spittle does not always work.'

We met no Saiyid beggars in Isfahan, though we saw a great many others, particularly blind beggars. Their numbers surprised me, but in the majority of cases they were not as blind as they appeared to be.

Abdul was cynical about beggars, especially blind ones. 'Some of them can see better than you can, Agha. And,' he added, 'it is well known that the Isfahani beggars are the most skilled in their profession in the whole country.' He said this with a touch of pride in his voice. Abdul was always ready to boost his own town.

A few days later, we actually saw an Isfahani 'blind' beggar plying his art, and his performance was of a surprisingly high order.

Abdul and I were strolling around some of the less frequented quarters of the town. As we turned a corner, we saw a couple of blue-gowned individuals in the middle of the road about seventy paces ahead of us. They had their backs to us, and were walking in the same direction as ourselves. They were conversing loudly and one appeared to have just told a funny story, for he slapped his companion on the back and both burst into loud laughter. They had not heard our footsteps in the powdery dust of the road, but one of them happened to turn around and caught sight of us. He nudged his companion and they immediately separated. One crossed to the right side of the road and stood against a big wooden doorway. The other quickened his pace and walked on.

As we drew nearer to the man standing by the doorway, an amazing change came over him. Moments before he had been laughing and joking, now he was hunched up in an attitude of complete helplessness and decrepitude. He was clinging to a heavy bronze knocker on the big wooden door, sobbing and wailing; tears were glistening on his cheeks and matted beard and his whole body was shaking, as though convulsed with grief.

He pretended not to have seen us approaching and I remained for several minutes gazing in astonishment at the extraordinary performance. His acting was superb. In Hollywood he would have made a fortune.

As we turned to go, the beggar called out in a broken imploring voice: 'Agha, *bibakhsheed* . . . Ali . . .' But Abdul came out with a flow of abuse: 'Begone, lose thyself, thou shameless son of a burnt father . . .' and we walked on.

'I feared you would give him *baksheesh*,' he said. And in another moment I probably would have done so, for if his blindness was not real, his acting certainly was.

Chapter 13

SOUTHWARD FROM ISFAHAN

The days in Isfahan passed all too quickly, and I was very sorry when the time came for our departure.

The bank manager's mechanic had given Zobeida a thorough check-up and greasing. She had so far behaved well and given little trouble. The last hilly stages before Isfahan had put a heavy strain on the brakes though, and their linings had worn very thin. I was unable to get any new linings in the town, so the mechanic tightened up the brakes and thought they would last for some time yet, but warned against getting them wet.

We made an early start and had already reached the outskirts of the city when Abdul pointed to a mud-covered pillar by the roadside.

'*Adem-i-getch*,' he said casually. With my attention concentrated on steering between two deep pot-holes, I did not give any thought to the remark, but subconsciously the words seemed familiar. '*Adem-i-getch*?'—and then I remembered reading about them—in Sykes's book, I believe.

'What was that you said, Abdul?'

'*Adem-i-getch. Unja.*' He pointed back. I stopped and reversed, and we got out and walked to the pillar. It was built of the usual sun-dried mud bricks, and originally it had been about the height and girth of a London letter-box, but had become weathered with the wind and rain of many seasons.

As Abdul began to explain, I remembered the meaning of *adem-i-getch*. It was the good old way of dealing with highway robbers. In Afghanistan the custom was to force the malefactor into a cramped iron cage, and suspend him from a tree or pole near the scene of his crimes. There he would be left to starve, as a warning to others.

The Iranians, more refined than the Afghans, immured their highwaymen by building a brick wall round them up to their neck, and then cementing them in with *getch* or quicklime, leaving only the head uncovered and thereby ensuring a slow and extremely unpleasant death.

The top of this particular pillar had crumbled away, but Abdul grubbed about with his fingers in the powdery dust and lime, and extracted what looked like a section of vertebrae. He held it out to me in the palm of his hand, then threw it on the ground and spat on it. '*Pider-i-sukhte*! He probably killed many people.'

'Do they still do this?' I pointed to the pillar.

'*Che arz kunam*,' he shrugged. 'Too much trouble to build the pillars. When I was a boy, there were plenty of these *adem-i-getch* along the roads leading out of town. Sometimes they just dug a hole in the ground and buried the thief up to his neck. Then they poured in the *getch*. But people would kick the heads—not so good—it killed them too quickly.'

'Come along,' I said, 'let's get on our journey.'

Besides its beggars, Isfahan is also famous for melons. The long green species known as *sardeh* resembles in shape and size a vegetable marrow, and is of a luscious sweetness equalled only by the melons of Turkestan.

The finest of all Iranian melons are said to come from a small town some little distance from Isfahan, called Gurgab. There is a legend that when fully ripe the melons are so tender and full of juice, that the vibration set up by the sound of a galloping horse a half-farsang away will cause the fruit to burst asunder. (The 'half-farsang' was Abdul's typical exaggeration but the story is well known.)

I had heard so much about the excellence of the local melons and of the custom of keeping them for months hanging in little grass cradles, that I wanted to purchase one to enjoy on the road. But it was too early for the new crop and the previous season's supply was exhausted. Abdul scoured the bazaars and finally found a single melon, which he assured me was the sole survivor in the whole of Isfahan. It was an unusually large one and, though slightly wrinkled after months of careful storage, it was otherwise in perfect condition.

When we left Isfahan, the weather was too cold to eat a melon with any enjoyment, so I packed it carefully away on top of the baggage at the back of the open car. For several days I resisted the temptation to taste it, preferring to wait until we reached the warmer desert country farther east.

Days passed. Often I gazed longingly at the melon and felt it carefully to make sure it was not getting bruised. Not yet! I kept telling myself. Better keep it just a few days longer, till we get down into the warmer region.

At last we arrived there. By mid-morning the temperature was soaring. Today's the day, I told myself. In one hour we would halt for lunch and eat the melon. There it lay, packed away on the baggage, carefully shielded from harm and from the sun.

The road had been very bad in parts, but the last few kilometres had been better. I was able to push Zobeida up to nearly seventy kilometres an hour. Then, without warning, disaster struck. It was the old story. Right across the road, and invisible until one was right on top of it, some *pider-i-sukhte* of a villager had dug a deep *joob*. There was no time to brake, even if the brakes had been any good, and they were not. The front wheels went down into the ditch with a frightening bang, nearly pitching both of us over the windscreen. As for the melon, it sailed through the air in a graceful curve, and landed with a sickening squelch some twenty paces in front of the car, in the middle of the road. I feared a broken axle, but by a miraculous stroke of luck the only damage was to the melon. It, of course, had burst into a million pieces.

I have digressed over the melon, because at the time it seemed a real tragedy, but in addition to that little mishap we nearly had a more serious accident.

Through the hilly country south-east of Isfahan I had driven Zobeida carefully, sparing the brakes as much as possible. At one place the bridge across a gully had collapsed from a recent flood. It had not yet been repaired, so I had to drive through the stream-bed with the water just deep enough to cover the axle and the wetting put my brakes completely out of action.

Having ascended another range of hills, I found the descent on the other side was long and gradual. There were no sharp bends and the road was visible and clear for a considerable distance ahead. At the bottom was a wide river-bed crossed by an unusually long and narrow stone bridge. When I was at the bottom of the descent I threw out the clutch and allowed Zobeida to coast down in neutral. When we reached the bridge she continued to roll smoothly across it.

I now saw that we were not alone on the bridge. Some distance ahead of us was a man on a donkey heading in the same direction as ourselves. He was already nearing the far end and I was certain he would be off the bridge before we caught up with him. I had switched off the engine; Zobeida was coasting silently along and, with diminishing speed, was gradually overtaking the man on the donkey. He was seated, oriental fashion, astride the rear end of the animal just over the tail. His legs were swinging in rhythm to the motion of the little beast, which was moving briskly along, sufficiently briskly, it still seemed to me, to clear off the bridge before we caught up with him.

We were now a mere fifty paces behind him. The distance lessened to forty, to thirty, to twenty paces. I put on the brakes as hard as I could, with no effect whatever. The man on the donkey was still oblivious of our presence, even when we came right up behind him. The force of the impact was so slight that he did not notice it. Probably he was asleep. Zobeida's radiator top was exactly level with the base of the animal's spine. The transition was so smooth that for a full moment or two the rider was unaware that he was now no longer astride the donkey, but seated astride Zobeida's radiator.

He heard us both shout, and looked round. Then, for the first time, he became aware of our presence. A momentary grin spread over his face, but the next moment it vanished and he gave a yell of astonishment as the heat from the radiator penetrated his thick baggy trousers. He leaped to the ground with surprising agility, then turned and laughed loudly as Zobeida came to a stop. But the laugh was only momentary. The next instant he gave a wild cry '*oolaghem! oolaghem!* my ass! my ass!' and flung himself down in front of the car.

With a fluttering feeling in the pit of my stomach, I climbed out. Horror! There, completely twisted and, it seemed, hopelessly entangled with the front axle and the gear-box, was the wretched donkey. Certainly he was dead and I began a hasty mental calculation as to the proper compensation for a dead donkey.

We got out the jack and raised the front axle as high as we could. Then we each seized a leg and pulled the animal free. For a moment or two he lay there, with his front legs seemingly where his hind legs ought to be. He was still alive, but I was sure his back must be broken, and I thought of getting out my gun and putting him out of his misery. But then, to my astonishment, the donkey began to unravel himself, and finally, with an effort, he staggered to his feet. A few minutes later, the amazing beast was contentedly cropping grass at the side of the road. We made a careful examination and found not only no bones broken, but not a single cut or blemish on the animal's skin.

The donkey called for no compensation, but when the man murmured something about his bottom being burned, Abdul let fly at him: 'Thy father was burned, and now it is thy backside. Who gave thee permission to seat thine arse on top of a *feringhi* motor!'

The man laughed good-humouredly and we both laughed with him. The fault was entirely mine and I was grateful to the donkey for being such a tough little beast. I gave its owner a few silver krans and we parted in all friendliness. As we started off, I looked round. The man was already back in his seat on the animal's tail-end, his legs swinging rhythmically as the donkey ambled merrily along.

*

Once the market-gardens and orchards of Isfahan were left behind the scenery continued drab and uninteresting for the whole seventy-kilometre stretch to Qumisheh.

'If there were more water,' I said to Abdul, 'all this land could be cultivated.'

Abdul was in one of his cynical moods. 'Without doubt, Agha, there would be more land to cultivate, but would the people be any happier for that?'

'Why not?' I asked.

'Remember the three 'Z's,' he said. 'In Persian we say that there are three main causes of human discord, namely *Zan* (woman), *Zar* (gold) and *Zamin* (land).'

'I think you have it wrong,' I said. 'Surely it was the other way round, and they are supposed to be the three main causes of human happiness.'

'*Nakhair*, Agha. Supposed, perhaps, but in truth there is more crime and violence over those three 'Z's than over anything else, except one thing . . .'

'And that is?'

'Water,' he said simply, 'because it is the key to all the rest.' He paused and looked at me doubtfully.

'I don't quite follow you.'

'*Bibineed*, Agha. You have just said yourself, "If this land had water . . ." But it has no water, and look at it. A wilderness, a *biaban*—of no value to any man. *Durust ast*?'

'*Durust*.'

'But with water, the *zamin* becomes a thing of value. A man can sell his produce for *zar*, and with the *zar* he can buy himself a *zan*. So you see the most valuable of all is water and there is more violence and crime and unhappiness over water than over all the three 'Z's together.'

'There's something in what you say,' I admitted.

'Something, Agha? You ask the *kedkhuda* (headman) of Qumisheh yonder. He'll tell you.'

All I could see in Qumisheh was a sprawling collection of squat mud-coloured dwellings, relieved only by the blue-tiled domes of several tombs, and the refreshing green of the surrounding vegetation. The village was situated in a small but fertile valley, and was fortunate in having ample irrigation. I felt no inclination to stop and ask the headman about village squabbles over water and we drove straight on, following the bumpy monotonous road for another long stretch to Yezdikhwast.

From a distance the town appears a very ordinary cluster of mud-walled dwellings nestling on the open plain. Only when one has approached to a few hundred paces does the bizarre character of the location become apparent.

My first impression, as I drove up close to Yezdikhwast, was that of a ship in dry-dock. For the town itself consists of a long narrow wedge of rock standing erect on its keel, as it were, in a dry river canyon.

The ship effect is enhanced by the fact that the rocky wedge is sharp at one end, suggesting the bows of a vessel. The top of it, houses jammed tightly together, rises crazily to a height of four storeys, resembling vaguely a ship's superstructure. The appearance of the town, if it can be called such, is even more striking when one descends into the bed of the canyon and looks up at the cliff and the buildings which seem to overhang it.

Seen by moonlight, Yezdikhwast could look like some fine citadel with massive protecting walls, surrounded by a great fosse. But viewed at close quarters in the glaring midday sun, the place, despite its unique position, is a picture of drabness and squalor.

One would suppose that a site with such natural defensive advantages must have been inhabited since very early times, but history has left no record of it. Abdul, who prided himself on his general knowledge, but whose facts were often curiously blended with legend and folklore, claimed to have knowledge of only one incident in the history of Yezdikhwast.

The villain of the piece was a one-time Governor or Vekil of Shiraz named Zekki Khan. This gentleman was an opportunist of no mean order, and when the death of the ruling monarch was followed by one of those periodic upheavals in which strong men are tempted to make a bid for power, Zekki Khan went into action.

He raised an armed following and marched on Isfahan. Yezdikhwast lay on his road, so he threw his troops round the town and demanded an exorbitant contribution towards campaign funds. When the citizens demurred, the Vekil had a number of the leading residents hurled to their death from the house-tops into the canyon.

Abdul embellished the skirts of his story with what was probably a little embroidery of his own fancy. He related that one of the victims had been a Saiyid, and a particularly holy one at that. Before being pitched overboard, the Saiyid just had time to utter some potent valedictory curses upon the Vekil and his men.

The Vekil retaliated by seizing the Saiyid's reputedly beautiful wife and young daughter. The former he threw to the soldiery and the latter he took to his own tent. As Abdul said, this was a great mistake and there was bound to be trouble. The total lack of respect for the sanctity of one of the Prophet's children was certain to bring down divine retribution. It did so, and very promptly.

That same night, while the Vekil was taking his pleasure in his tent, a fifth-column of outraged Yezdikhwastians penetrated his camp and cut the Vekil's tent ropes. He was a very fat man, and as he floundered about in the folds of the canvas like a fish in a net, the citizens set upon him with their knives and threw what was left of him down into the canyon to join his murdered victims.

I checked up on the story later and found there was some substance to Abdul's version of the incident, which happened in 1779, but little else seems to be known about the history of the place.

The only outstanding building in Yezdikhwast is a caravanserai, whose ruins lie slightly beyond the town and bear the unmistakable hallmark of its Safavid builders.

The road leads down into the canyon-like ravine and skirts the cliffside, the old houses clustered above with their crazy wooden balconies, like swallows' nests overhanging the ridge.

I left the car in charge of Abdul to discourage the local children, who at once came crowding round, and started off on foot, seeking a spot down in the ravine from which to get the most effective photographs. I told Abdul to hold the attention of the youngsters, so that I could steal unobtrusively away, and he did this by letting the little ragamuffins amuse themselves with the horn. Numerous adults with time hanging on their hands thronged round to join the fun and I was able to get my photographs unmolested.

A Don Quixote might have pictured the sunbaked canyon as a medieval moat surrounding some baronial stronghold, but for me all romance faded when I came upon the decomposing carcase of a donkey, and the air became filled with a nauseating stench and a myriad carrion flies.

In attempting to give the carcase a wider berth I walked in closer under the cliffside, which was the town wall, and the next moment without any warning a shower of garbage came pelting down, missing me by inches. It might have been intentional, probably was, but it provided a practical demonstration of the use of the urban defences as a common refuse dump.

This was not my first experience of Iran's ancient city moats and drains. Some years earlier, in Khorasan, I had arrived at the outskirts of the country's most holy city, Meshed, late at night after a long and tiring journey. After traversing mountain trails since daybreak, I had trudged the last few miles on foot, leading an equally exhausted pony. Groping in pitch darkness along a considerable stretch of the old city ramparts, I mistook a breach in the wall for a side gate into the city. While trying to drag my unwilling beast through the gap, the wretched animal slipped and we both rolled down into the bottom of the deep city fosse, which was also by common usage the municipal refuse depository.

For a quarter of a mile I continued to grope through indescribable stench and foulness, until I finally clambered out just beside the main city gate. My sudden appearance from the depths of the fosse and utter blackness, dragging my pony behind me, sent several timid citizens scurrying in panic. Their shouts of alarm brought the *tufangchis* at the gate rushing out, and in the general excitement they concluded that I was a thief who had stolen the pony, and impounded both me and the animal.

After Yezdikhwast (which means, incidentally, Desire of God) the first village of any size along the road was Abadeh. Here the presence of a tea-house gave us a pretext for a brief stop. The owner, or perhaps he was the manager, was a friendly soul and greeted us at the entrance. He was not a big man, but he had a disproportionately big head and this was crowned by an outsize black felt *kulleh.* In shape it looked like an enormous inverted pudding basin, and reminded me of an ancient Egyptian I had seen carved in relief in the Abu Simbel temple.

After greetings there followed the usual question and answer.

'What is there to eat?'

'Everything that your Honour wishes.'

'But what?'

'*Chae, churek, tukhm-i-murgh, wa mast.*' (Tea, bread, eggs, and curdled milk.)

I was hungry enough to have eaten everything and it was on my lips to answer *'hameh che dareed'*, meaning 'the whole works'. But Abdul warned that we were approaching Dehbid, which, 'as your Honour knows', is the coldest place in all Iran. Your Honour did not know, but Abdul's argument that it would be wisdom to eat a hot meal in Dehbid, and escape a while from the bitter mountain wind, seemed to make sense, so we contented ourselves in Abadeh with a glass of tea and a cigarette. Outside, the sight of a donkey drinking from the *joob* made me think of Zobeida and I filled her radiator from the same source. We took the road again and soon began the long steady climb to Dehbid, Village of the Willows.

It was at this stage that Abdul caught a chill. As it turned out, I made a mistake in following his advice to push on and eat in Dehbid rather than in Abadeh for, as Abdul had warned, it was bitterly cold in Dehbid and it might have been better to have passed right through there without stopping. Dehbid is 7,500 feet above sea-level. We made the long ascent driving into the teeth of a whistling head-wind which got stronger and colder as we advanced. By the time we got to the top of the ridge, we were both chilled to the bone. My hands and feet were numb, and with Abdul swathed in his shabby old sheepskin kaftan, we stumbled rather than walked to the entrance of the unpretentious little tea-house.

The air was thick with charcoal fumes from a big brass samovar and two or three glowing braziers, but the acrid odour was softened by the savoury aroma of boiling rice and frying chicken. We ordered a meal of this and washed it down with glass after glass of hot tea. An hour later, with a pleasant warmth tingling in my veins, I was ready for the road again.

Abdul, on the other hand, felt sluggish and was reluctant to leave the smoke-filled, over-heated tea-house. He would have liked to remain there all night, but I was anxious to get as far as we could before nightfall, because next morning I planned to spend time visiting the site of ancient Pasargadae and also Persepolis.

The cold became less as we drove down the long descent, but Abdul sat bundled up in his old sheepskin and remained unusually quiet. As we reached level ground, we startled a small group of gazelle grazing by the roadside. They kicked up a series of miniature dust-devils as they bounded away across the open plain, to vanish in the growing dusk.

A few kilometres farther on I sighted the figures of three men ahead of us on the road. They were carrying weapons and I instinctively slowed down and nudged Abdul. For a moment or two I thought of stopping and taking out the gun, but Abdul, after peering doubtfully at them, gave a reassuring grunt. They were militiamen without doubt, but from their ragged appearance and slouching gait they might have been stragglers from some nomad encampment or just plain robbers.

When we came up with them they shouted out a loud and friendly *salaam aleikum*, I stopped the car and they crowded round asking the usual questions. 'Who are you? Where are you going and where are you from?' With their scrubby, unshaven but smiling faces, they looked like the Iranian counterparts of the Three Musketeers. They told us they were a road patrol and their duty was to protect the highway from thieving nomad tribespeople. We said we had not seen any so far, but they told us there were several encampments in the neighbourhood. They warned us not to drive through the dark and advised us to spend the night near their outpost, about a kilometre along the road ahead.

I offered them a lift and in a flash the three of them had piled themselves atop the baggage, with their legs dangling out of the car. We stopped at their outpost, which was a small square *burj* or tower, just off the road. They urged us to spend the night there, and as they were so friendly and it was getting dark already I drove Zobeida off the road and parked her in the shelter of the post.

The militiamen dragged up a pile of cut camel-thorn and got a fire started. The fuel blazed and crackled, but some of it must have been either green or damp for it gave out a lot of thick smoke. With much coughing and spluttering they succeeded in bringing a large open pan of water to the boil, and brewed some very smoky and acrid-tasting tea.

We turned in early and the next morning I presented our militiamen friends with some tea, sugar and cigarettes. They were as delighted as schoolchildren with a box of candy, and they waved us on our way with a chorus of *Khuda Hafiz*.

Abdul definitely was under the weather. He had a temperature and remained huddled in his sheepskin. It looked to me like a bout of malaria, probably brought on by a chill caught in Dehbid. An hour later he was shaking with ague and so, without turning aside to look at Pasargadae, and with a pause at Persepolis just long enough for me to mount the great stairway and descend it again, I drove straight on. Soon we reached the famous gateway of Allah-U-Akbar, overlooking the city of Shiraz, with its tombs and gardens sprawled out beneath us.

Chapter 14

SHIRAZ

In Shiraz I made at once for the British Consulate and Chick, the Consul, an old friend, welcomed me and insisted on my staying with him. The Consulate Mirza undertook to look after Abdul. The local doctor confirmed the fever as malaria, dosed the patient with quinine and confined him to bed.

Chick had spent much of his service in Iran, and spoke the language with unusual fluency. He was one of those popular Englishmen—Sir Percy Sykes was another outstanding example—who had lost their hearts to the country and its people, and had earned the reputation of being 'more Persian than the Persians'.

For such a character Shiraz should be an ideal place to live in, for it prides itself on being the most purely Persian of all the cities of Iran. It is the capital of the southern province of Fars, the ancient Pars, from which came the very name Persia. Perhaps it is only natural therefore, that as Abdul so often assured me, 'the sweetest Persian is that spoken in Shiraz'.

The very early existence of the town is veiled in the mists of mythology, but with the Achaemenian royal cities of Pasargadae and Persepolis only a short distance away one would assume there must have been some settlement in such a favoured position. Traces of two fire-altars show that the town existed at least in Sasanian times and it is recorded history that during the initial Arab invasion the Arab forces made Shiraz their base of operations against the Sasanian capital of Istakhr, whose ruins are not far from Persepolis.

However, compared with many other Iranian cities Shiraz is not rich in ancient monuments. It has one really old mosque, the Masjid-i-Jami, which dates back to the eleventh century. There are also two highly decorative and relatively modern mosques, that of Saiyid Ahmed (eighteenth century) and the Shah Chiragh Mosque, built early nineteenth century.

Shiraz is better known for its tombs of famous people and also for its gardens. Among the tombs, there are two sixteenth century mausoleums, both marking the resting places of prominent women of their period, but the most famous tombs belong to two of Iran's greatest poets, Sa'adi and Hafiz. Both were natives of Shiraz. Sa'adi was born in the late twelfth century and lived to a ripe old age, and Hafiz was born only a few years after Sa'adi's death. Both tombs were restored during the eighteenth century, when the gardens surrounding them were also replanted.

So much has been written, both in prose and in verse, about the gardens of Shiraz, that one is inclined perhaps to expect too much and the very name Shiraz is suggestive of bulbuls (nightingales) and roses. I saw a number of gardens, and inhaled the fragrance of red roses, but failed to hear any nightingales. Such gardens as I saw were poorly tended but their ill-kempt lack of formality had a charm all its own, particularly in the late afternoon. Then, the dark spire-like shafts of the cypress, contrasting with the tender green background of young poplar and willow foliage, were reflected in the mirrored surface of a lily-pond, while overhead the cloudless western sky magically turned to magenta and the surrounding bare hills to a delicate lilac.

I could feel the enchantment of Shiraz, and I would have liked to stay there longer, though not solely for the nightingales and roses. I would have liked to visit at leisure the great Achaemenian ruins that I had missed on my way down: Pasargadae, Naqshi-i-Rustom, Persepolis, Istakhr, and the Sasanian carvings near Qazerun, all within easy reach of Shiraz and covering one of the most eventful historical periods of the ancient world.

So far as my own work was concerned there was really nothing to keep me in Shiraz, but I had planned to make a side-trip down to Bushire on the coast. I was disappointed to learn that this was not immediately possible, as heavy rains had caused subsidences and landslides, which had blocked several stretches of the road.

I knew Bushire of old, but I had never seen the hinterland between the coast and Shiraz. At the best of times, the road had the reputation of being one of the most difficult in the entire country. Except for the immediate neighbourhood of Bushire, between which and the hills there is a low-lying expanse of swamp called the Mushaila, the road consists of a giant switch-back, or rather a series of switch-backs, rising in one lofty mountain range after another. The passes are known as *kutals*, and the highest and most difficult of them are the Kutal-i-Pir-e-Zan, or Pass of the Old Woman, and the Kutal-i-Dukhtar, or Pass of the Daughter. I never could find out the identity of the old woman or her legendary offspring.

Despite advice not to attempt it, I decided to try to get as far as the Pir-e-Zan and back. Abdul was out of circulation, so I went alone. It was well that I emptied everything out of the car to lighten it, for otherwise Zobeida would not have made some of the steeper ascents. It was not that the gradients themselves were so difficult, but as a result of the recent heavy rainfall, the slopes were thick with slimy mud and in terrible condition.

Zobeida was not the only motor vehicle attempting the journey that morning. There was one other, a Chevrolet truck which had been converted by a local craftsman into what was supposed to be a bus, though, apart from having been fitted with windows, it looked more like a hen-coop on wheels. The entire bodywork threatened to disintegrate on the slightest impact, while the tyres had lost all trace of tread and looked just ready to burst. But the owner evidently took some pride in his creation, for the body had been freshly painted a vivid green dotted with bright red roses and above the windscreen was a board neatly inscribed with a girl's name, Shireen.

I came up behind this contraption as it was attempting one of the first really steep gradients after leaving Shiraz. It was a particularly bad stretch of road, with the hillside rising steeply like a wall on the right, at the foot of which a fairly deep drainage ditch had been cut. The rains had filled this with semi-liquid mud. On the other side of the road, the hillside dropped away abruptly into the valley below, and to make matters really difficult, at this particular point the rain had washed away a considerable slice of the highway. The road surface was a sticky morass, possessing all the viscosity of the best East African cotton soil. As Zobeida approached and skidded to a halt, Shireen was skating wildly from one side to the other, her engine racing and wheels flaying up the liquid mud in all directions.

All at once she swerved violently, swung through an angle of ninety degrees, and came to a dead stop as her nose hit the steep mountainside and her front wheels sank into the mud-filled ditch, leaving her rear wheels with only a few inches between them and the crumbled edge of the cliff. The road was completely blocked.

Shouting wildly, the passengers came tumbling out of the bus. There were about a dozen of them altogether, including the driver and two women, also a couple of goats and some hens tied together by the legs. The men crowded round the vehicle and began noisily to discuss the situation. Unable to drive past, I waited, curious to see what would happen next.

The driver of the bus was clearly at a loss to know what to do. The passengers obviously did not know either, but took the view that, since he had got them into the ditch, it was up to him to get them out of it. All he had to do, they argued, was to go into reverse and drive out backwards. To this he pointed out the obvious fact that if he did reverse and extricate the front wheels, the rear ones would inevitably go over the cliff and possibly the whole bus would follow. This temporarily silenced the opposition. Someone now suggested that the *feringhi* might have some solution whereupon they all appealed to me.

Together we examined the front wheels. They were embedded half-way up to the axle in thick mud. 'You'll have to jack them up and put stones underneath,' I told the driver. He shrugged, shrinking his neck tortoise-fashion between his shoulder-blades. 'But Agha, we have no jack!' A chorus of groans went up. 'He has no jack!' 'Allah help us!' Meanwhile the two women remained bundled in their black *chadors* inside the bus, together with the goats and the hens.

The driver appeared receptive to any suggestions, so I advised him to collect some large stones and pieces of rock. Fortunately there were plenty about and this was soon done. Next we detailed several men to grip the front right wheel, and when the driver shouted 'Y'Allah', to lift it all together, while others pushed stones under it. After one or two failures, they succeeded in extricating the right wheel from the mud, and then they repeated the operation on the other front wheel.

The driver now regained some self-confidence and began to take the initiative. First of all he sensibly lightened the bus by ordering out the two women and removing the goats, hens, and a pile of miscellaneous baggage. Next, he instructed the male passengers how to push the body of the vehicle so as to swing it round parallel to the ditch. He then got back into his seat and gripped the wheel, while the women and I and the goats stood clear and watched the operation.

The passengers now showed a commendable team spirit. They put their heads down, braced their shoulders against the bus, and awaited the word of command. The driver yelled Y'Allah!, and the crowd put their backs into it with all the ardour of a rugger scrum, heaving with all their strength. Something had to give way and it was Shireen. She swung away from them so suddenly that half of them fell flat on their faces in the mud. The remainder, carried away by their own enthusiasm, continued to push until, with a crash and tinkling of broken glass Shireen stopped dead, hard up against the hillside. The impact did something to the wiring of the horn, which began to blare protestingly and refused to be silenced.

Unable to switch off the horn, the driver switched on the engine, but this, with diabolical perversity, refused to start. A chorus of groans and imprecations went up from the crowd, for now, instead of Shireen having her nose and two front wheels in the ditch, she had her left front and left rear wheel in it, with her body hard up against the hillside. What was worse, the vehicle was now pointing north instead of south, back towards Shiraz instead of towards its destination, Bushire.

At least the road was open. I had lost much valuable time, but there was nothing I could do to help so I drove on my way, leaving Shireen with her horn wailing faintly as the battery began to weaken, while the angry passengers cursed and burned the driver's father.

The road continued bad in many places. Zobeida boiled furiously as she struggled up the long gradients in bottom gear, and several times I thought I would never reach the top of the pass. But the view from the summit was worth the effort, and I was rewarded with a grand panorama of bare brown mountain ranges decreasing successively in height, until they dwindled to mere foothills and lost themselves in the coastal haze of the Persian Gulf.

On my way back I saw no sign of Shireen, other than a patch of broken glass where she had hit the hillside, and a surrounding area of trampled mud. Evidently they had abandoned the venture, to struggle back home the way they had come.

Back in Shiraz I began to prepare for the onward journey. My next objective was Kirman, and although Abdul was now recovering from his malaria, he made it clear that even if he were physically fit he would never venture further east from Shiraz. It was bad country, peopled by robbers and cut-throats. Worse than that, it was a land accursed and fraught with every kind of danger, both natural and supernatural. He warned me of a long list of frightful things that might happen to me, and insisted that any Shirazi who agreed to accompany me must either be mentally afflicted or a scoundrel, and would assuredly let me down, if he did not actually cut my throat.

Abdul's concern was genuine, but he was never of the stuff that heroes are made of and his relief was great when I paid him two extra months' wages and sufficient for the road back to Isfahan. Meanwhile the Consulate Mirza was having difficulty in finding any local man to take his place. Chick positively refused to allow me to go on without a servant or companion. We had a difference of opinion also, as to which road I should take. He urged me strongly to make the long detour by way of Yezd, though he admitted that the more direct route through Niriz was much shorter and reputedly in better condition. It had been partly repaired by British army engineers during the war years, but when the troops left it fell into disuse. No telegraph line ran along it, and there were no militia posts or any form of protection. Robbers were said to infest it and altogether it had a bad name.

The Yezd road would be much safer, Chick insisted, but the time factor had begun to weigh heavily with me. From Kirman I planned to go on to Meshed. This meant another long journey through mostly uninteresting country which I had traversed some years earlier, and I was anxious to get it done while Zobeida's tyres were still in reasonably good condition. I pointed out to Chick that, since the southerly road had fallen into disuse, there would be little to attract robbers, and in the end he gave way. He had given me sound advice and if I declined to take it then he would wash his hands of me. 'All I can say is,' he concluded, 'whatever you do, keep clear of Niriz. It's a notorious nest of robbers, and you'd better get past it as soon as you can.'

At last the Mirza found a man to replace Abdul. His name was Hassan, and he was a tough-looking character who claimed to have served with the military mechanised transport. In support of this, he produced a torn and very dirty discharge certificate, of which the greater portion was missing. He claimed to know all about motor-cars, and in addition he said he knew the road to Kirman. He seemed to have the very qualifications I needed and I was by this time so anxious to get started that I omitted to ask a good many questions that should have been asked. I overlooked his rough uncouth manner and engaged him then and there.

Abdul wept real tears when it finally came to parting. He repeated his earlier warning that, in tempting Allah, I would surely come to a sticky end. If the robbers or the *djinns* didn't get me, or the desert engulf me, something else equally unpleasant would definitely overtake me and the vultures would have me in the end. It all seemed so unnecessary, he wailed, that the hands which had fed him so generously should end up feeding carrion birds.

I had had Zobeida thoroughly overhauled and new brake linings fitted. In addition to a full tank I carried four extra four-gallon containers of gasoline, also one full tin of lubricant. I continued to carry two large containers of water as well as the two canvas *chagals*. I made Hassan load up Zobeida the night before in readiness for an early morning start. 'Now remember what I told you about Niriz,' was Chick's final warning. 'Good luck, and you'll probably need it.' I started Zobeida and we drove off, an hour later than I had planned.

Chapter 15

ORDEAL OF THE HASSANABAD PASS

Hassan was a disappointment from the beginning. He was surly, he never smiled, and he seemed to be perpetually brooding over something. Abdul would probably have suspected him of possessing the evil eye, for things began to go wrong from the very start.

We had barely covered ten kilometres, when the right front tyre gave a long-drawn hiss like an angry serpent and went flat. Three inches of donkey-shoe had sliced into the inner tube. I helped Hassan jack up the car and change the wheel. This he did clumsily and with very bad grace, muttering imprecations on all donkeys, and burning the parents and grandparents of their owners. By the time we had gone some sixty kilometres it occurred to me that the sun was not in the place it should have been. We were heading in the wrong direction. Despite Hassan's protests that he knew the road and that we were on course, I insisted on turning back, and we wasted another full hour before we found the right road.

Much worse was to happen, for about ninety kilometres from Shiraz I noticed that the engine was overheating badly. In hill country Zobeida's radiator boiled continuously and to all appearances she might have been running on steam, for her absorption of water was as great as her consumption of gasoline. But this was not hilly country. I checked the oil level and found it dangerously low. I had told Hassan to fill up with fresh oil the evening before, but had carelessly omitted to check it myself. Now I told him to bring out the new can of oil I had purchased in Shiraz. Hassan moved to the rear of the car and went through the motion of opening and rummaging about in the boot. There was an ominous silence, then, 'Agha, *framosh kardem*, I forgot to bring it.'

The surprising thing is that I didn't murder Hassan on the spot. As it was, I blew up and burned his father and his father's father until they should have been in cinders. But it didn't help matters. It was the engine that was in danger of burning. We had to wait and let it cool down and then drive slowly with occasional stops. Our only hope now was Niriz. Perhaps we could get some oil there. But Niriz was the one place Chick had warned me to keep away from.

We reached there well after midday. It was a dirty-looking town, and so were its inhabitants. The first thing I saw was the rusty skeleton of an ancient car. Its bones had been stripped clean of every movable part, but the mere presence of the old relic raised a glimmer of hope that we might find some motor lubricant in the place.

I called for the *kedkhuda*, the communal headman. He was a shifty-looking individual and the throng that came along with him looked worse, but perhaps I was prejudiced. He shook his head. They had no *roghan* for the motor. The only *roghan* they had was local mustard oil. I pointed to the derelict car and the headman explained that a stranger had driven it from Shiraz a long time ago. He had taken one of the Niriz merchants for a drive and the merchant had been so impressed that after a lot of haggling he bought the car. The stranger pocketed the money and left. But the merchant had overlooked one thing—a motor needs fuel. No fuel was to be had in all the country around. The car was finally pushed into the ditch and quickly picked clean by scavenging villagers. And there the skeleton still lay.

I bought a can of raw mustard oil and reluctantly poured some into the engine. Then we left Niriz as quickly as possible. We had lost much valuable time and the afternoon was already far advanced. But at least the motor continued to run, despite the mustard oil.

We drove on through a landscape completely dead. The whole of this region was impregnated with salt, which glistened in the sun like a heavy fall of snow. Away ahead of us, a range of rocky hills stretched down from north to south, and the map showed that we would have to cross them by a fairly high pass. In the clear light of late afternoon, with the sun directly behind us, the hills looked no more than a dozen kilometres distant and I hoped to be across them before dark.

But as we drew nearer to them I could see they were further away than I had thought and much higher than they appeared from a distance. Also the road now became very stony and began to climb, as we approached the foothills.

I found it increasingly difficult to follow the track, which had been washed away in many places, necessitating long and time-consuming detours. The sun had already reached the horizon, and the rocky range now rising immediately in front of us proved to be mountains rather than mere hills, and presented a formidable barrier to our progress. We could never reach the top of the pass before nightfall.

For a few minutes the range stood out, a vivid magenta red in the dying rays of the sun. Then the magenta turned to pale purple and finally, to bluish grey. Soon the colour faded and it seemed as though a dark curtain had suddenly descended upon the whole landscape. The track was no longer distinguishable and after blundering on a little farther I realised that we had lost it. I switched on the headlights, or rather I tried to switch them on, but nothing happened. They refused to work.

I jumped out to locate the trouble. With Hassan peering over my shoulder and holding the camp lantern, I fiddled about with the wiring. I invoked Hassan's expert help, but he now admitted he knew nothing about batteries or electricity. I failed to locate the trouble, and since it was clearly useless to continue groping our way among the rocks and thorn bushes, there was nothing for it but to halt for the night where we were.

Hassan now came out in his true colours. He protested that we could not possibly stay there. It was dangerous; the hills were infested with robbers. Their look-out men must have seen us, and we would almost certainly be attacked during the night and have our throats cut. We should turn and go back to Niriz.

'Niriz? Never,' I said. 'We stay right here.'

For a moment Hassan glared at me over the flare of the lamp. He muttered something about it being madness. He knew these people better than I did, and if I wanted to have my throat cut, well, that was my affair, but he would not stay. Before I realised that he meant it, he turned and walked off into the darkness in the direction from which we had come, taking the lantern with him.

I was so surprised, I made no move to stop him. I expected him to think better of it and come back, but he did nothing of the sort. I watched the flickering light of the lamp—my only lamp—finally disappear in the distance.

Now I was alone and in complete darkness. I made another fruitless attempt to find the fault in the lighting system and then gave it up. There was no moon and I hoped that the dark shape of the car would not be visible against the shadowy background of the mountains. But the stars came out with startling brilliance in a cloudless sky and anyone passing along that way could not fail to see Zobeida. Moreover, one could be quite certain that anybody who did happen along there late at night would certainly be up to no good.

I fumbled about in the provision box and found a tin of corned beef and a can opener. Then I drew my shotgun from its case and slipped half a dozen buckshot cartridges into my pocket. I put on my old trench coat, for a cold breeze was blowing from the wide expanse of salt flats.

Next, I found a large thorn bush some thirty paces from the car. I collected rocks and built a low breast-wall, such as on the Frontier is known as a *sangar*. Then I loaded the gun and laid it down carefully beside me.

It was difficult opening the can of corned beef in the dark, but the spare battery of my flashlight had run down and I had to do the best I could. In any case, a light might have attracted unwelcome attention. By the time I had eaten the meat I felt much better and prepared to receive visitors. I kept myself awake by thinking up all the Persian terms of abuse and the biting phrases with which I would greet Hassan if he dared to show up again, although I half hoped that I had seen the last of him.

It must have been about two o'clock in the morning when I was awakened from a doze by the sound of footsteps over the stony ground. At first I thought it might be Hassan returning, but soon I spotted a group of moving shadows.

They stopped and I heard them muttering among themselves. They were not more than forty paces from the car and they must have seen it.

My hands went quietly to the gun. I didn't want to start a row, but I was determined not to let them approach the car. Also I did not want them to think that I was completely alone. I began to mutter and to laugh to myself aloud, just loud enough for them to hear. I continued mumbling and laughing, trying to create the impression that we were a group of people.

Now was the critical moment. If they started to spread out, I would have a fight on my hands, for that would mean an attempt to surround me. Fortunately, they did not; they remained grouped together. Seemingly, they were puzzled; there was the car—and somewhere, at a distance from it, people were talking and laughing. It did not make sense. Since the people were laughing, they clearly were not afraid.

Gaining confidence myself, I took a chance and came out with a really loud guffaw. I followed it with a still louder Ha'Ha'Ha! In the darkness it must have sounded weird. Crouched behind my *sangar*, I was invisible and they could see no movement. I even began to enjoy the situation.

Iranis are notoriously superstitious folk. These people were certainly up to no good, prowling about at that unholy hour. Probably their nerves were on edge. Possibly they concluded they must have run into a whole nest of *djinn*. There was some loud muttering and in a matter of moments they had melted away into the dark.

I managed to keep awake until daybreak, but no more visitors came along. As soon as the first pallor showed up the rocky crest above me I searched round and quickly found the road. It was rough and stony and overgrown with thorny scrub, but it was unmistakably a track. I unloaded the gun and packed it away in its case. Then I lit the pressure stove, brewed myself some tea, and chewed a piece of stale *churek*. I still thought that Hassan might turn up, and spent a little while checking the wiring of the headlights until I found and repaired the break. Then I packed the stove away and as there was still no sign of Hassan I started up the engine and got the car back onto the track, to begin the long gradual ascent which led right up to the foot of the range.

Zobeida seemed to run satisfactorily on the mustard oil, but the real test was yet to come. I could see the road snaking up and up in continuous bends, disappearing from view only to reappear much higher up on another flank of the mountain.

Trouble began only too soon. On the next gradient, a much steeper one, the motor stalled on the actual bend. From this point onward the road was so narrow that Zobeida could only just scrape by with her wheels on the brink of a drop of several hundred feet. The sun was now well up and its rays were beating down mercilessly on the rocky track and the barren treeless slopes. There was not a scrap of shade anywhere.

Zobeida would now only move forward in bottom gear and, even so, she kept grinding to a stop every few score yards. Finally she refused to start, and I was compelled to reduce the load. The heaviest items came off first. These were the four gasoline containers and the two containing water. With these dumped by the wayside, Zobeida went off with a dash, but on the next bend but one we ran into serious trouble and had to stop dead.

This was a particularly difficult corner, where the mountainside dropped away abruptly into the valley. There had been much erosion, and a big slice of road had broken away, leaving a gaping space where the ballast and debris had rolled down the hillside. This was real trouble and it was impossible to pass.

The obvious solution would be to fill in the gap with rock and rubble. Luckily there was plenty of this available, but the difficulty lay in piling the material together so that it would stay firmly in position. My fear was that the whole flimsy repair job would crumble and go down the hillside immediately any weight was applied.

To reduce the risk as far as possible, I off-loaded all the heavier articles of baggage. Then I got into the car and crawled forward in bottom gear, praying the engine would not stall. Half-way across the rubble began to slide and Zobeida heeled over. I held the door open in readiness to jump, but the engine kept going, we pulled out safely and the worst was over. Or was it?

We rounded the next bend and there, fifty metres away, lying exactly in the middle of the road and blocking it completely, was an enormous boulder. Here at last, it seemed, was journey's end.

A mule or a donkey could have squeezed past, but certainly not Zobeida. That the heavy boulder should have come to rest right in the middle of the track was just diabolically too bad. Was this really the end? I could not even reverse, for without ropes and assistance I could never re-cross that corner with the gaping hole. I had passed the point of no return. I sat down on a rock to rest and try to think things out calmly.

Was there any likelihood of anybody coming along that way? So far I had not seen a living soul. At one or two places I had noticed mule or donkey droppings and some of sheep or goats, but they were all old. Human help therefore seemed a remote possibility. I could only pray and hope for a miracle.

Supposing I abandoned the car. I would then have to sacrifice all my kit and everything I had with me. I could carry my gun, a water-*chagal*, a few tins of provisions, and foot it à la Robinson Crusoe, either back across country to Niriz, or avoid Niriz and risk the salt marshes in an attempt to reach Shiraz. Alternatively, I could push on and take my chance of finding some village ahead. I had better take a good supply of ammunition for either game or robbers.

Zobeida had by now ceased to boil violently and was gently simmering. I had a careful look at the boulder. I estimated it must weigh about half a ton. It was irregular in shape, but the outer side was roughly rounded. Then I had an idea.

There was a space of only three feet between the boulder and the edge of the slope. If I could break away sufficient of the road to undermine the boulder, it might start rolling again and crash down the hillside. Then I could fill in the hole again and drive over it as I had done at the previous bend.

The idea seemed feasible. I inspected the ground beneath the boulder. It was hard and solid. A pick would have done the trick, but I had no pick. The nearest thing to it was the jack-handle. It was a poor substitute but, *faute de mieux*, it would have to do.

For a full hour I worked away. Within the first five minutes my hands were skinned and bleeding, and I had made little impression on the road. However, once I had prised away one or two lumps of rock, the rest came more easily, and then at last I began to undermine the big boulder itself.

I stripped off my sweat-soaked shirt and vest, and wrapped them round my bleeding hands. Then I continued to pick away, and carefully piled up all the loose rock and rubble on one side to refill the cavity. I tried pushing the boulder, but could only move it just a very little. Then I had a better idea. I bolstered the jack itself firmly against the rear of the boulder. With a few turns of the jack handle the big rock began to tilt, then with a few more turns it suddenly toppled over and crashed into the ravine far below.

I was tired out and dripping with sweat, and my hands were a mess, but I managed to push enough rubble into the gap in the road to fill it. Then I got into the car and drove on without difficulty. Now came a shorter but particularly steep gradient and Zobeida refused point-blank to take it. This time there was an air of finality about the manner of her stopping which savoured of the camel and the last straw.

There was nothing else to be done. I took every single remaining article out of the car, including the spare wheel and the back seat, and dumped them by the wayside. Then I jumped in, started the engine, and we moved slowly forward.

Yes, we moved forward—and move was just the proper word to describe it. Zobeida was now as light as I could make her and I had hoped she would make a dash for it. Instead, I just managed to keep her crawling in bottom gear. On the next bend she laboured badly and I feared that the mustard oil might be largely responsible. I was almost desperate, for if she stalled now it would probably be final, since there remained nothing in her to unload except myself. The engine began to knock painfully. A few more moments and she would stall. I jumped out and ran alongside, one hand on the wheel and the other on the open door, steering with one hand and pushing with the other.

Mercifully, Zobeida picked up a little momentum, and now it was I who was labouring, as I was half-dragged breathlessly up the steep incline, hanging on to the steering wheel and the door and trying to keep her on a straight course. I was on the inside of the road and could not see the outside edge, but I knew that there was only at best twenty inches' and in many places a mere six inches' safety margin to the brink.

I would have given anything for a rest and for something to eat and drink, but everything was down below and if I wanted it I would have to go and get it. There was no shade to rest in. I had recovered my breath, so I started down the hill.

Four-gallon cans, each containing 15.2 litres of liquid, whether inflammable spirit or just plain water, are not intended to be carried any distance by hand. They have a thin wire 'handle' by which one can pick them up, but the wire quickly cuts into one's hands. I had foreseen this and on the way down I had taken a stout strap from my bedding roll. I passed this through the handles of two of the containers, then slipped it yoke-fashion over the back of my neck. Part of the strain was taken by my neck, and with my raw blistered hands still wrapped in my shirt and vest, I was able to carry two containers at a time.

But it was a painful operation; the wire soon began to cut into my hands, the strap chafed and blistered my neck. Also the tin containers were burning hot from having been lying in the blazing sun all day. I handled them carefully, indeed timidly. Perhaps it was my imagination, but they seemed to be bulging ominously and I carried them with the haunting fear that if one of them sprang even the smallest leak, I would immediately go up in flames.

The gradients seemed very much longer and steeper on foot than they had appeared in the car, but I gradually carried up all four gasoline containers as far as the corner where I had mended the gap in the road, and where the other heavier articles of baggage were lying. But there still remained the two heavy containers of water glinting tantalisingly in the sun nearly a kilometre below me. There was nothing for it and down I went again. My hands were now so cut and raw that, rather then endure the pain of carrying the whole eight gallons, I poured away most of the precious water, leaving only about a gallon in each container.

I now treated myself to lunch, consisting of a very warm can of tongue, and another of peaches supplemented by a piece of stale native cheese which I did not recognise, and assumed must have belonged to Hassan. But my enjoyment of the meal was marred by one completely baffling problem. How on earth was I ever going to get this mass of baggage up to the top of the pass?

To an observer the performance must have appeared as mad as it was comical. Looking back on the scene from above, I wondered how I ever made that steep grade without going over the edge. Again and again the wheels must have been grazing the very brink, and not for the first time in this venture with Zobeida, I had felt that God was very near.

And so we made it safely to the following bend, but by this time my heart was pounding louder than Zobeida's cylinders and my legs were dragging badly. I felt that if I could just keep her going until we had rounded this corner, I would have to halt for a rest, even if it meant never starting again.

We just got round it, and immediately we had done so, I sensed the difference. The gradient ahead was a long one and less steep, but the altitude we had now reached began to affect my breathing. Panting till my lungs felt like bursting, I pulled myself wearily back on board, as Zobeida began to pick up speed. Then, to my unbounded relief, the actual shoulder of the range came into sight. In a matter of minutes we reached the top of the pass. I thanked God that we had actually made it. But who were we? Just Zobeida and myself. The car was a mere empty shell, and it now remained to pick up the pieces I had left behind.

Pick up the pieces exactly described it. I got out, sat down on a rock, and quickly jumped up again as it burned through my thin slacks. The sun's rays poured viciously down upon the surrounding mountain crests. Below me I could follow the line of the road, coiling like a giant serpent round the contours of the hills, now disappearing behind a rocky spur, now reappearing on the distant flank of a deep valley.

Far away down in the main ravine something glittered in the sunlight. It might have been the reflection from a stream of water, but it was not. I knew only too well what it was. It was my gasoline and water containers, the first things I had dumped, now separated from me by a long zig-zag pattern of back-breaking mountain track. At another point, not visible from where I stood, were several bulky suitcases, the stove and heavy provision box, and some distance farther up again, the spare wheel, the back seat and the tool kit.

I could see no immediate solution. To carry up everything in one continuous operation was clearly beyond my strength. If I started in at once, I could not possibly complete it by nightfall. Since it seemed highly improbable that anybody would come along, I need fear no interference and could do it in gradual stages. I had my shotgun, I could remain on the hillside as long as my provisions lasted, and then the very heavy food-box could be jettisoned.

The only alternative solution would have to be a miracle.

I felt rested and better after the food, and I decided to begin moving again. My hands were too sore to carry the gasoline, so I selected a couple of suitcases and started up the hill with them.

Half-way up the first gradient I paused for a rest, and peered up at the hill-tops to see if I could count the remaining gradients to the summit. Then I saw something which made me catch my breath with excitement.

It was moving slowly down along the road, but was so far

distant that it was barely visible against the brown colour of the background. I could make out the figure of a man, then those of several men. My first thought was for my gun, since it seemed incredible that anybody on that hillside could be there on lawful business. My field-glasses were with the rest of my kit, but I kept my eyes on the distant figures. I could make out three men and some animals, either mules or donkeys. They might be honest *charvadars* and my hopes rose—or they could be robbers with stolen animals. I dared take no chances. I carried my suitcases back down the hill and got to my gun as quickly as possible.

I had plenty of time to reach my dump before the party would round the last bend and I did some rapid thinking. If they were robbers, I might be in for trouble, but if they were honest folk this might be the miracle I had prayed for. At all costs I must get them to help me. As a precaution I dragged all the baggage onto the road itself until I had effectively blocked it. Now, whether they wanted to or not, they would have to stop.

As the party approached down the slope, I could see that the three men were not armed, and they had the appearance of ordinary *charvadars*. I counted ten donkeys, and none seemed to be carrying any burden. The men stopped and halted their animals when they saw me. They returned my greetings civilly, though somewhat nervously, owing probably to the sight of my gun and the pile of baggage on the road.

They told me they had been alarmed at the sight of the deserted car at the top of the pass, also the spare wheel and the back seat lying by the roadside. They said the pass had a bad name and they were anxious to get clear of the hills before nightfall.

I promised them a good reward to carry my baggage to the top and after some hesitation and argument, for they appeared genuinely frightened, they loaded all my stuff onto their donkeys and headed back up the mountain.

We picked up the remaining articles on the way and in a very short while the entire baggage had been deposited around the car. I chatted with the muleteers and gave them some cigarettes, and by the time we reached the top we had become so friendly that they even helped me to load up Zobeida. I paid them the agreed reward and they thanked me and hurried on their way as fast as their animals could go. I filled up the radiator from my remaining water supply, and gave the engine a further dose of mustard oil. Away in the distance I could just discern Niriz, surrounded by a shimmering expanse of salt, and in sharp contrast looming up from the haze behind it a line of jagged, dark basalt peaks.

Once over the shoulder of the pass the descent was long and gradual, but the road was bad. In several places the track had been washed away and I had to search round for a detour. Over long stretches I had to grope and pick a way through wide patches of eroded hillside. Some distance down towards the plain I reached a small village with a ruined caravanserai. It was not much to look at, but the smell of wood-smoke suggested food and shelter, and I was in need of both. I halted and parked Zobeida in the lee of the old serai.

The headman of the village, a fine-looking old man with fierce, penetrating eyes under shaggy eyebrows, an enormous beak of a nose, a beard dyed fiery red with henna, and a patriarchal Old Testament air, came out with a handful of followers. My arrival by motor-car out of the blue could not have caused more surprise than if I had glided down by space-ship from Mars.

Their astonishment was all the greater when they saw I was a *feringhi*, and travelling without servants or retainers of any kind. One of the villagers incautiously placed his hand on Zobeida's glittering radiator cap and let out a yelp of pain. There followed much stroking of beards and muttering of *wah! wah!*

Radiator caps have a fatal fascination for the unwary. I remember once, on an Assam tea plantation, an elephant impelled by curiosity made the same mistake. But the elephant took it badly. He lost his temper and smashed the car to pieces.

The headman was a friendly old character and insisted on my accepting his hospitality. He said something about killing a goat and making a pilau, but I declined and we compromised on tea, boiled eggs and freshly baked bread. The tea especially, tasted unbelievably good. I had been sweating continuously all day and must have been nearly dehydrated. I drank glass after glass of the sweet amber liquid and ate a full half-dozen hard-boiled eggs.

During the meal the headman plied me with questions about the road. Had I met the three men with the donkeys? I said I had and told him how they had helped me. He wagged his head. They were wise to carry no merchandise, he said, because there was a band of robbers roving the hills. Only a few days previously they had beaten up some shepherds and taken their sheep. Nowadays, very few people carried weapons. He said I had taken a very great risk and warned that it was foolish to be travelling alone. I replied with the usual comment that Allah takes special care of fools and this brought a laugh all round.

The headman offered me the shelter of his house and when I insisted on remaining with Zobeida and my baggage he told two villagers to spend the night near me for my protection.

I could not refuse this, but I thought it well to mention that I had a gun and enough ammunition to keep off any band of robbers. This casual remark produced more beard-stroking and murmurs of *wah! wah!*, but it probably dispelled any tempting thoughts some of them might have entertained.

I spent the night rolled up in my blankets at the side of the car, with nothing to disturb my slumber until the loud braying of a donkey awakened me to the reality of another day.

The headman pressed upon me as a parting gift a supply of hard-boiled eggs and *churek*. He refused payment, but was glad to accept some cigarettes in exchange.

The remainder of the journey to Kirman, like so many stretches on this long trip, was uneventful and uninteresting. The only striking feature of the landscape was the number of *kanats*, those astonishing underground tunnels which convey water from the foot of the hills to a town or village lying miles away in the open and otherwise waterless plain. Viewed from the surface, the countryside appears to be dotted with hundreds of giant molehills, spaced at regular intervals and stretching in long straight lines, sometimes a score or more kilometres in length, from the distant foothills.

Each molehill marks the mouth of a clean-cut rectangular shaft sunk down to the level of the underground tunnel, and serving both to ventilate it and to enable the *kanat*-diggers to make periodical inspections and to keep the water channel clean and unobstructed.

The *kanat* system of irrigation is very ancient and the profession of *kanat*-digger a skilled and honourable one. Its secrets are jealously guarded and passed on from father to son, and one may often come across quite tiny youngsters descending with a rope to inspect and clean out the underground channels.

Chapter 16

KIRMAN

In Kirman I was unfortunate in finding the Consul away on leave, but the Consular Trade Agent, Mr Muinzadeh, an Iranian, kindly offered me the hospitality of his house and I gratefully accepted. Also through his good offices, I met several of the leading notables and local merchants and spent much of the first two days visiting and talking with them. Then with my own business disposed of I felt free to take time off for some sightseeing.

Since my arrival the weather had been disappointing, with the sky heavily overcast and the air laden with fine powdery dust. However, on the third morning I was awakened early by the sun streaming into my bedroom and from my window I looked out onto a typical Kirman garden. Unlike romantic descriptions by Sa'adi and Hafiz, there were no nightingales singing, and no beautiful maidens culling lotus blossoms. Instead, there were a few cypress and poplar trees, some roses, and a blue-tiled *hauz* of water. One had to draw upon the imagination for the rest. A shrouded female figure squatting by the tank and washing a pair of *shalwar* might quite possibly have been a beautiful Persian *houri* with rosebud lips, cheeks like peaches, and gazelle-like eyes. Might have been, but wasn't, for I had unfortunately caught a glimpse of her face.

Framing the garden were the inevitable high mud-plastered walls and beyond these, forming a striking background, was the lofty ridge of hills which borders immediately on the town. Crowning the ridge, now purple against the awakening eastern sky, the battlements and crenellated walls of an ancient stronghold descended towards the confines of the inhabited area of the town.

At breakfast I mentioned the ruins, and learning of my interest in ancient monuments my host offered his services as guide. We therefore set out together on foot, and I was surprised at the extent of the ruined areas. They appeared greater than the existing town itself.

This is not so strange when one considers that the history of this whole part of the country is one long chronicle of invasion and massacre, destruction and rapine, also that from here onwards towards the Afghan border the entire region is a savage wilderness, ravaged by man and nature, with only an occasional oasis to relieve its sterility. No wonder Abdul refused to venture east of Shiraz. I could see now why he believed the civilised world to end there. He would have hated this environment.

Our first objective was the stronghold, standing out stark against the skyline. We were walking through ruins almost from the centre of the town and thence followed a rough track along a dry water-course up to the crest of the ridge, some five hundred feet above the town and the surrounding plain. The fortress is known as the Qaleh-i-Ardeshir. My host and guide professed himself keenly interested in ancient history, though I did not really believe him and thought he only pretended this out of politeness. He assured me that the great fortress was three thousand years old. It certainly had been an impressive and important stronghold, for it had three separate lines of defence, and the walls were constructed of unusually large sun-dried bricks, which were surprisingly well preserved. The structure was undeniably very ancient. It might well have been built by Ardeshir, the first Sasanian monarch, whose name it bore, or, judging by the solidly laid stone foundations, it might have been originally of Parthian construction, dating back possibly to the first century AD, though certainly not three thousand years. In close proximity were the ruins of a second fortress, known locally as the Qaleh-i-Dukhtar, and probably also of Sasanian construction.

In Iran all mud ruins look alike, and it is often difficult to say whether they are one hundred or one thousand years old. Indeed, it is often not at all easy at first glance to distinguish between weathered ruins of sun-dried brick and natural formations of the terrain. But while it is difficult to fix a definite date for Kirman's numerous ruins, they bear eloquent testimony to the region's tempestuous past. Although, unlike the majority of Iran's larger cities, Kirman escaped the wholesale devastation inflicted by the Mongol invasion of AD 1220, and without going back beyond the Sasanians, whose empire was overwhelmed by the rising tide of Islam and was finally extinguished at the battle of Nihavand in AD 644, the long Arab occupation was followed by a steady succession of invaders: the Seljuqs in the early eleventh century, then the Turks and Mongols, Tamerlane and the Timurids, followed by the 'Black Sheep' and 'White Sheep' Turkman. Then, after a period of relative peace, in 1722 Mahmud of Ghanzni captured the town, followed only seven years later by Nadir Shah. Hardly was Nadir dead, when Ahmed Shah Duranni swept down upon Kirman, and laid waste the entire Zoroastrian section of the town. As the Afghans left the area, so it remained on my visit.

But the last and worst of all the periodic scourges was Agha Mohamed, the first of the Qajar line. He turned his troops loose upon Kirman, and gave them three months in which to ravish and pillage to their hearts' content. When this orgy was over, he sold twenty thousand of the survivors into slavery and ordered the commander of his troops to blind another twenty thousand of the inhabitants, and bring their eyes to him to be counted.

The Turks had a superstition that it was unlucky to rebuild on the site of a house that had been destroyed. I asked Muinzadeh if a similar superstition prevented the Kirmanis from rebuilding their ruined areas. He smiled and shrugged, '*Che arz kunam*!'

Kirman has many mosques, but few of outstanding architectural merit. The oldest is the Masjid-i-Malik, built in the late eleventh century. The Masjid-i-Shah was built half a century later. The Masjid-i-Jami' dates from the mid-fourteenth century and the Masjid-i-Meidan from about the same time.

But the only monument with a pretence to real beauty is the Shrine of Ni'amatullah at Mahun, a few miles outside Kirman.

Ni'amatullah was greatly respected as a descendant of the Imam Bakr, and was born in Aleppo in 1330. He had a thirst for learning and was a persistent traveller. He acquired additional merit by spending eighty days in solitary meditation on the frozen summit of Mount Demavend, Iran's highest peak, through one winter. On one of his longer journeys he followed the 'Golden Road' to Samarkand, where he was entertained as a guest by Tamerlane himself. Tradition has it that Tamerlane became somewhat uneasy at his guest's growing popularity and influence and, in the hope that he might desist from his constant peregrinations, the monarch ordered an attractive residence to be built for him at Mahun. Here, the saintly old gentleman founded an order of dervishes and after putting in still more travel he died in 1430 in his 101st year. After his death, a shrine was built at Mahun by his numerous devoted followers. It was surrounded by a fine garden, still attracts devotees, and ranks among the most beautiful shrines in Iran.

I drove out to Mahun, but arrived there only shortly before dusk and was therefore unable to see the shrine or garden at their best.

Apart from one interesting feature, the Kirman bazaars have little to distinguish them from those of any other Iranian city, except that they are perhaps more dilapidated than some, and much less picturesque than those of Isfahan, Tehran, or Tabriz. The noteworthy feature is that the women of Kirman traditionally wear white *chadors*, instead of black or dark blue, as worn almost everywhere else in Iran. I was unable to find out the reason for this distinction, which seems to date back a considerable time.

Carpet-weaving is still the main activity, though it has long ceased to be a purely local craft and has been commercialised and organised by foreign interests on a large scale. In general care has been taken to preserve the ancient quality of craftsmanship despite the enhanced scale of production, but the big companies have taken over existing native looms, not only in the town of Kirman, but also in a large number of the surrounding villages. The ancient method of weaving has therefore remained the same, and continues to be carried on mainly by women and young children, while introducing new designs and colour combinations to meet the prevailing tastes of the western markets.

It has always puzzled me that people living in such dreary and uninspiring surroundings are able to produce the brilliant and intricate designs of their famous rugs and carpets.

As in other Iranian towns, it is a common practice to spread newly woven rugs down in the bazaar roadway, to be covered with dust and dirt and trodden underfoot by men and animals. It says much for the enduring quality of both craftsmanship and materials that the rugs appear to suffer no injury. Indeed, the treatment is calculated to subdue the harsher colours of modern dyes in the newly woven fabrics, while giving them the sheen and patina which are supposedly only acquired by old age.

Chapter 17

THE LAND THAT ALLAH FORGOT

From Kirman my plans were to travel up to Meshed in Khorasan, and thence turn back westward to Tehran. I was not looking forward with great enthusiasm to this part of the journey, for I had covered most of it before and there were long stretches of uninteresting country. At the same time, I was not sorry to be leaving Kirman. I was sure that if I had some definite occupation there, had I been the consul or the bank manager, or connected with the carpet industry, I would probably have become attached to the place and its people and of course its ruins. But I missed that charm which had appealed to me strongly in both Isfahan and Shiraz and felt that a few days' stay here was quite enough.

I was just finishing writing up notes for my next reports when, to my great surprise, Muinzadeh knocked at my door and handed me a telegram. It was about the very last thing I expected. To me Kirman seemed remote and isolated from the outside world, and I had forgotten the existence of the telegraph. Here, suddenly, came a reminder. And the contents of the telegram were a still greater surprise. It was from the board of directors. They thanked me for my last batch of reports and requested me to proceed as soon as convenient to India, to look into their existing organisation there, and in countries further east. I should advise them when I eventually reached Bombay.

This sudden development was as welcome as it was unexpected, and had happened most opportunely, since it absolved me from the long and monotonous trek up to Meshed. Now the question presented itself, how should I 'proceed' to India? Normally this would mean returning to Tehran, then down the road through Kirmanshah to Baghdad, thence to Basreh and by sea to Bombay. As I subsequently learned, this is what the directors in London assumed I would do.

The thought occurred to me of going through Afghanistan. This had long been a dream of mine, but I discarded the idea at once as impracticable. Permits would be necessary, and to procure these would entail much delay. This would be entirely inconsistent with 'proceeding as soon as convenient' to Bombay.

There was just one alternative. I could bypass Afghanistan and reach India 'by the back door' by continuing eastward from Kirman. This seemed to be the obvious solution, for to me it appeared ridiculous to go all the way back across the Iran plateau, when the road ahead would be so very much shorter.

True, there was still a considerable expanse of notoriously bad desert stretching eastwards from Kirman through Mekran, but once I reached the border of Beluchistan I would be on familiar ground. Some years earlier, I had covered the whole distance from Beluchistan to Khorasan—over six hundred miles of some of the most desolate country in Asia—partly on foot, mostly by horse or camel. At least I knew the kind of ordeal that would face me. And apart from anything else there was a challenge about the venture which appealed to me—I just could not bring myself to turn back, with this tract of unknown country luring me on.

When I told Muinzadeh of my idea he shook his head. He admitted he knew nothing of road conditions, but he thought the undertaking would be extremely hazardous for anyone to embark upon alone. He promised to make immediate enquiries in the town and did so, but he failed to find anyone in Kirman who had reliable knowledge of the road beyond the first stage from Kirman to Bam. Next morning we tried again, but all we could learn was that beyond Bam the road was most difficult, dangerous and well nigh impassable. Several people even declared that there was no road at all, only the *biaban*, the wilderness, while some of the more canny ones looked at Zobeida with a disapproving eye and shook their heads. 'In that old rattle-trap,' they said, 'it would be sheer madness to try.'

But I still had faith in Zobeida. I knew her many weaknesses, but everything likely to go wrong had already done so and had been fixed. The compression in the engine was not too good, but no serious damage seemed to have resulted from the severe test she had undergone while running on crude mustard oil.

Muinzadeh had strong misgivings about letting me go on alone but he had no power to stop me, and he had to admit that since I had got through so far safely there appeared no particular reason why I should fail to complete the journey.

I delayed an extra day to give Zobeida a careful overhaul, and this time I drained out the sump myself and filled up with good fresh lubricant. The people in Kirman were right and I met with no difficulties on the first stage as far as Bam. In fact I covered the distance so much quicker than I had expected that, after halting to brew some tea and eat the usual meal of *churek* and boiled eggs, I took time off to pay a quick visit to the old fortress itself. The entire original town of Bam was enclosed within a high defensive perimeter wall protected by a deep ditch, much of which had fallen in. Entrance was by a main gateway. The massive wooden doors were still hanging on their rusty iron hinges and were secured by a heavy chain, but there was just sufficient gap between them and the ground for me to squeeze through. Inside were lines of crumbling buildings and the remains of a bazaar. Behind, in the background, were the battlements and the main keep of what must once have been an impressive stronghold.

I walked through the mass of ruins until I came to the main structure. The entire area appeared completely deserted. Apart from some wild pigeons nesting in the ruined bazaar, a pair of ravens perched on one of the upper ledges of the main tower, and the occasional lizard basking on a crumbling wall, I saw no signs of life. The pigeons cooed mournfully and the ravens croaked hoarsely from their lofty perch; otherwise the silence was complete. I found the desolation depressing and even began to sense a feeling of uneasiness.

It was just around midday and the hot sun blazed down from a cloudless sky. From the top of the tower every corner of the whole area would be visible and I could not detect any sign of movement amid the adjacent ruins.

A wide ramp, flanked by a loop-holed curtain wall, wound upwards round the base of the main tower. It was an easy ascent and I started to make it. As I reached the upper section of the tower my approach disturbed the ravens, who took to the air and circled overhead with angry cries.

The view from the top was worth the climb. Immediately below was the ruined area and beyond the outer walls the surrounding plain spread out flat and arid as far as the eye could see, except in the east, where a blur of distant mountains loomed up vaguely through the haze. It was not a landscape to hold the attention, but a monotonous expanse of mud-coloured terrain, sprinkled with thorny scrub and a sage-like type of bush, its surface here and there intersected by dried-up water-courses.

Of human life within the walled ruined area I saw no sign, and indeed the entire surrounding landscape appeared completely deserted. But the feeling of unease persisted. I thought of the car, standing unattended by the entrance gate. It contained all my belongings, including my cameras and my gun. Unwise to leave it so long unprotected and I felt a strong urge to get back to it quickly. On my way down the ramp I noticed an open doorway leading into the interior of the tower. I distinctly heard the sound of some movement inside, but could only discern a passageway leading into complete darkness and I hurried past. Just as I reached the bottom of the ramp, the ravens, who had quietened down once they observed me retreat, broke out again into loud angry croaking. I moved across from the inner to the outer side of the ramp and as I did so, with a dull thud, a piece of coping from an upper ledge crashed down on the ramp immediately behind me. I glanced quickly upwards. The ravens were circling and croaking loudly. Something had disturbed them, but I could discern no other movement. Yet something or somebody must have dislodged that piece of coping! It was too close an escape to be pleasant and I tarried not one moment further, but hurried straight back to the entrance, squeezed myself hastily through the gap under the heavy wooden doors, got into the car and drove away as quickly as I could, without pausing to get out the camera and take a few snaps of the fortress as I had planned.

A few miles beyond Bam I met a party of *charvadars* with their mules. I stopped to pass the time of day and get some information about the road ahead. I mentioned the old fortress at Bam and asked if anybody still lived in it. They shook their heads and said the place had a bad name and honest folk kept away from it. They said there had been several recent robberies in that neighbourhood, and a few days earlier some travellers had been killed and their goods and animals carried off.

Regarding the road ahead they said there had been violent rains and in many places the track had been washed away, also that in the Shurgaz area strong winds had piled up sand dunes and obliterated the trail. They warned me on no account to stray from the road, and with mutual wishes of *Khuda hafiz* we went on our respective ways.

I was now right out in the country I had seen from the tower of the fort—a stone-covered plain with no vegetation other than camel-thorn and rough scrub, with here and there a clump of stunted tamarisk, *gaz*, the natives call it. As I progressed further patches of wind-driven sand occurred with growing frequency and later appeared in the form of dunes.

The *charvadars* had not exaggerated. I had been carefully following what had started as a well-beaten track, eroded at intervals by flashfloods which had carved out deep channels and had then dried up, leaving no trace of where the track had been. At such places all I could do was to cast round in a wide circle until I came upon the trail, only to lose it again where it had been buried by other stretches of drifting sand.

I had had plenty of warning that the road would be

difficult, but I had not counted on it disappearing altogether. To make matters still more complicated, I now discovered that my map was hopelessly vague where this particular tract of country was concerned and I could no longer rely on it. I blamed myself for not having included a compass in my kit, but it would probably not have been of much help, since I could not consistently follow any fixed course, but had to go where the going was possible, even if it meant long detours and deviation. Several times I found I had been following what I believed to be a track, only to find that it ended up in a sandbank.

This happened again and again as the afternoon wore on and the sun sank steadily lower. As the light began to fail, I realised that instead of isolated sand dunes I was now on the fringe of a vast expanse of real desert, stretching away into the distance ahead. I also realised that I was far off my proper track and was lost in no-man's land.

There was only one thing to do—make a halt, boil some tea, dig into my provision box and camp for the night where I was.

Immediately the sun dipped below the horizon, the temperature dropped, and a chilly breeze came sweeping across the desert. As the wind got stronger, it picked up the sand and grit and propelled it with a shrill whistling sound through the air. Tiny, sharp-edged particles rattled on the windshield and the bodywork of the car, and stung my face and hands until I took shelter under the heavy tarpaulin which served me as a tent.

The wind continued to blow all night and only died down with the rising of the sun. By that time I was almost buried in sand. It had seeped underneath the tarpaulin and penetrated my clothing and trickled down my neck. The car was full of grit and what was more serious the storm had obliterated the previous day's wheel-tracks. Now, as the sun rose over the great dreary void, it seemed that I was completely cut off from the outside world. The wind had died away, but just as the temperature had gone down with the sun, so the two now rose again together.

Despite the storm in the night, I had managed to get several hours' sleep. I awoke as the first faint pallor appeared in the eastern sky. After a cup of tea, hastily brewed on the camp stove, I felt again ready to tackle the problems of the road ahead. In the fresh pre-dawn air these no longer seemed as serious as they had the night before. Zobeida appeared none the worse for the sand-blasting she had received. I had plenty of fuel and water. My food supply was sufficient to see me through to India. And so as the first fingers of dawn reached up from behind the ranges of Beluchistan, I started up the motor and the two of us, Zobeida and I, headed into the sunrise across the sandy waste.

This was very different from the Syrian desert. There the terrain was hard and the only dangers lay in blundering off the trail in a sandstorm, or becoming separated from the convoy and being attacked by roving Bedouin. This desert presented quite a different problem. In appearance it was very deceptive. The surface was completely flat and smooth, not undulating like many of the other sandy tracts I had already crossed. Also it was covered with fine gravel, so fine that it was difficult to find a pebble with a diameter greater than a couple of inches. I discovered this later when I tried to collect a quantity of them to place under the wheels.

But the gravel itself proved to be only a thin veneer. The sand underneath was soft and powdery, almost like fuller's earth, so that one could push one's fist straight down almost to the elbow. Though I had not suspected it, there were areas in this desert that were dry powdery quicksands.

Soon the wheels were dragging badly. I stepped hard on the gas and tried desperately to keep the car moving. It was no good, the engine pinked and came to a halt. I got out, brushed the sand away from the rims and got Zobeida moving again. But I had had a warning and I realised the danger. Supposing I got really stuck and failed to pull out? There would be no likelihood of anybody coming along and helping me. Even the Beluch and Sarhadi tribespeople avoided this region during the dry season, for there was neither water nor grazing; no subsistence for man or beast.

It was a discomforting thought but, minutes later, as I succeeded in getting rolling again, I consoled myself with the assurance that of course it could not happen to me.

And then, forty-five kilometres further into the heart of the desert, it did happen. It was already mid-morning. The sun beat down mercilessly. The metalwork of the car blistered my hands when I touched it; the back of the seat burned through my shirt. I managed to keep the saliva running in my mouth by sucking a pebble, but felt I was becoming dehydrated.

The stops became more frequent and the runs shorter. Zobeida no longer had the same pull. The radiator boiled continuously and I kept adding fresh water. This was almost boiling already when I poured it out of the kerosene tin, and the container itself was so hot I had to wrap a cloth around it before I could pick it up.

The procedure became a routine. The wheels would drag, the engine would stall. I would get out, clear the sand from the wheels, climb back into the car, start the engine, slip in the clutch and drive forward one hundred, or occasionally with luck even two hundred metres. Then once again the wheels would drag to a halt and the whole miserable performance had to be repeated.

The last time this happened, there was a suggestion of finality about it. I even imagined that Zobeida gave a sigh and then a groan, as the motor stalled and she settled down like a worn-out camel in her bed of sand. Very discouraged, I climbed out and inspected the rear wheels. We had got into a softer patch than usual and their rims were buried much deeper than on previous occasions.

I did not know how many more kilometres the desert extended, but with this snail's rate of progress, I began for the first time to wonder whether the water supply would last out, or for that matter whether I myself would last out. I began to feel very tired.

It was nearly noon. I had eaten nothing since early morning, and then only a bit of *churek* with my cup of tea. 'Keep your head,' I told myself. 'Better eat something before any further exertion.' I got out a large piece of *churek*, and after eating this and a couple of hard-boiled eggs, washed down with a drink of hot and muddy water from my canvas *chagal*, I felt better and got down to work.

For the next two hours I sweated in the burning heat, trying to get Zobeida out of the sand and into action. I tried every trick and device I could think of. Time and time again, after laboriously digging away the grit from the rims and spokes of the wheels, with a prayer I started the motor, but each time the same thing happened; the rear wheels whirred round and buried themselves deeper in the powdery sand. Again and again I jacked up the rear axle, then filled in the ruts and tried to make a fresh start, but always with the same result.

Then I tried collecting stones to lay under the wheels to give them something to grip, but it took a lot of walking and searching, with bent back and the blazing sun beating on the back of my neck, to find even a handful of pebbles. And when I laid the miserable collection beneath the tyres and started the motor, the wheels immediately ground the pebbles into the sand.

Next I began to off-load the car. I had not tried this earlier for the obvious reason that, supposing I did manage to pull the empty car out of the sand, how was I going to reload it again without bogging down and finding myself no better off than before?

I off-loaded in stages, lifting out first the cans of fuel. Then I tried starting the motor and throwing in the clutch. No use. Then out came the suitcases. Still no use. Then the rest of the baggage, every bit of it, including the spare wheel and the tool-kit, but it was all fruitless; the rear wheels merely spun round and ground themselves still deeper into the sand. I tried placing the heavy tarpaulin under the back wheels, but they caught it up as though it had been a piece of calico, and twisted it so tightly round the rear axle that it took a long time and cost me much sweat and exertion with the aid of the jack to free it. I even removed the seat cushions and tried putting them under the wheels, but they were immediately whirled away as the tyres caught them.

Then I tried one more trick, the last in the bag. I started the motor while standing beside the car, then slipped in the clutch and rushed round behind and tried to push. I tried this a number of times, but it was all in vain. For the second time on this trip, Zobeida was stripped clean of everything movable. She was now as light as I could make her, but she was still far too heavy for me to lift unaided. I had no more tricks to try. By this time the wheels were buried up to the hub-caps and with every further movement they burrowed still deeper into the powdery quicksand.

With all this effort, I had developed a splitting headache and was becoming exhausted. Also I was seriously worried. I remembered Abdul's warning about deserts that engulfed people. Perhaps he knew more than I had given him credit for. Perhaps there were such things . . . Perhaps this was one of them . . . Nonsense. Keep your head! I kept telling myself. Take it easy! There's no need to panic. Of course there's a way out, only you haven't hit on it yet . . . there's damn well got to be, I thought, but what the hell is it?

Once more I scanned my surroundings. Emptiness—complete emptiness. I could see no horizon. I could not discern where earth ended and sky began. I could see only the dancing heat-waves and the quivering mirage. I had a splitting headache. God, how it ached. Could it be heatstroke? Keep calm, I kept telling myself.

I lay down beside the car, and drew the heavy tarpaulin over my head and body to get what shade I could. I shut my eyes tightly to ease the throbbing in my head and tried to reason things out calmly.

I must have fallen asleep, but was awakened in a brusque and startling manner by what sounded like a rifle-shot.

It took me a few startled moments to realise that I was not dreaming, and a few more to satisfy myself that there was nobody in sight. Only then did I discover what had awakened me. The explosion was real, but it had not been a rifle-shot.

Nor, thank God, was it the fuel-tank, nor the spare container of gasoline that I had carelessly left unprotected in the blazing sun. It was the tyre on Zobeida's right front wheel.

This was serious enough, for the burst was a bad one, and marked the end of that particular tyre. I would now have to fit on the spare wheel, but as I stood contemplating the casualty an idea occurred to me. The burst tyre offered a broad flat surface to the sand. Supposing I deflated the other three tyres . . . perhaps . . . perhaps . . .?

Minutes later I had partially deflated the remaining tyres, leaving just enough air in to protect them from the rims. Then, with a prayer on my lips I started the motor and threw in the clutch. There was an agonising moment as the rear wheels spun round, and then they gripped. Zobeida lurched forward and we began to move. Almost afraid to breathe, I gently accelerated. We pulled out of the ruts and moved ahead. I changed into second gear and we moved ahead still faster. With a feeling of indescribable relief and thankfulness I had got Zobeida going. But now I was afraid to bring her to a halt for fear of getting bogged down again. Several times I drove in wide circles round the piles of baggage, in search of a patch of harder sand. Slowly, fearfully, I brought her to a halt and got out. The half-inflated tyres barely indented the surface of the desert!

Eureka! I had found the solution, and wondered why I had not thought of it before. I soon had Zobeida loaded up again, then without even waiting to brew myself a much needed cup of tea and ignoring my headache I drove off, with the afternoon sun already behind my back. Now that the whole outlook had changed and Zobeida and I were back in circulation, the situation seemed to be once more under control. As the sun sank lower, above the blurred mirage ahead of me I could discern the clearer outline of distant hills, but elsewhere at ground level I could see nothing except dancing waves of heated air. In every direction but one. Away, half-right of me, I could just make out a darker blur floating on the sea of mirage. At that distance it might have been a tree, a camel, or some form of structure, but whatever it was it did not seem to have any right to be isolated out there in that vast expanse of emptiness. I decided to investigate and changed course in its direction.

Distances are deceptive in the desert, especially with the mirage playing tricks with one's eyesight. The object quickly became more distinct, though still ethereal and seemingly suspended in air. Minutes later it resolved itself into a solid body in the form of a lofty circular tower, rising some sixty or more feet from the surrounding desert, like a red brick lighthouse in a mud-coloured ocean.

I made sure it was uninhabited before I approached too close, and then I remembered having read about it in some early travel book. It was an ancient watch-tower built on a still more ancient caravan route. On some large-scale survey maps it is dignified by the name Mil-i-Nadiri, or Nadir's Column, printed in archaic type. There seems to be no reliable record of when it was built, or by whom. Some authorities date its construction around the tenth or eleventh century, and it must have been standing there in its desert solitude for many centuries before Nadir Shah came on the scene. To me the sight of it was most gratifying, for it enabled me to correct my bearings and fix my onward course with a fair degree of certainty.

Chapter 18

BELUCHISTAN

The deflated-tyre technique seemed to put new life into Zobeida, and we rolled steadily across the remaining miles of desert without further hold-ups, other than occasional stops to fill the fuel tank and replenish the water in the radiator, which boiled away merrily and continuously.

I halted at sundown and cooked myself a meal. Since the worst of the soft sand now appeared to have been left behind, I spent some time pumping up the tyres again. I did not inflate them fully in case there might be more sandtraps ahead. Besides, pumping was hard work and I preferred to do it in stages. I also replaced the wheel with the blown-out tyre and now, with no spare left, I could only pray that there would be no more bursts or punctures.

Next morning broke fine and I made an early start, with the hills now standing out clearly ahead of me. As the day advanced a bank of dark clouds began to form on the eastern horizon, and continued to build up until they filled half the sky. Over the distant ranges I could see the occasional quivering of lightning, and could hear the faint rumble of thunder. Ahead of me numerous dust-devils came twirling along, and I thought of Abdul and his tales of *djinn* and *afreet*. They whirled past me, pursued by a blast of cooler air, which swept up the dust and grit and bombarded the windscreen in a warning of trouble to come.

The distant rumbling soon turned into a growling; the very grandfather of a storm was brewing in those hills. Worse than that, it showed every sign of moving down to meet me in the open plain.

I began to think of shelter. The desert was becoming less even, its surface broken by *rudkhanehs* or stream-beds. Some of these were just shallow depressions, others were deeper with well-defined banks. I came to one of these deeper ones now. At a point a little further down, a group of tamarisk bushes had obtained a roothold and overhung the bank. It was not much of a shelter, but at least it offered some protection from the gathering sand-storm.

I found a place where I could descend into the dry stream-bed and manoeuvred Zobeida as close under the bank with the tamarisks as I could. Down there we were at least protected from the force of the wind and could wait in the lee of the bank until the storm blew itself out. I decided to profit by the enforced halt to brew some tea and eat my lunch.

I took out the pressure stove and had just got it burning when there was a flash of lightning, followed a few seconds later by a crashing peal of thunder. Up till then the quivering and rumbling had been distant, and I had hoped it would remain over the hills. But now it was much louder. The storm was not yet overhead, but it was already down in the plain and approaching rapidly. It was clearly going to be a violent one, and after my experience in the Syrian desert I had no desire to be caught in the open and buried in sand.

It was getting much darker and the wind was rapidly gaining force; it whistled furiously through the tamarisk branches just overhead, and blew my stove out. There was another vivid flash, followed almost immediately by an ear-splitting crash and crackling. And then I heard a different sound. For a moment I confused it with the rattle of the sand and grit, but it was more like the patter, patter, patter of thousands of little feet. I thought of the migration of the lemmings and the flight of desert marmots before an oncoming storm.

But when a heavy spot of rain splashed on my hand, followed by several others on the windshield, I knew what it was. Now I could not only hear it, I could smell it. From lemmings my thoughts flashed to a scorching day in the Punjab plains. For days heavy storm-clouds had been piling up, and one could smell the approaching monsoon long before the skies opened and the deluge began. Now again I could smell the rain; it was not a sand-storm after all. The dust was only a warning prelude. I threw the still hot stove into the car, jumped in myself, and began to edge Zobeida out from the bank into the open stream-bed. I knew the danger.

I remembered an occasion on the frontier, when one of my patrols was crossing a dry river-bed. It was deeper than this one and had a rocky bottom. There had been a cloudburst in the hills, though we did not know it at the time. The storm did not come down to the plain, but the floodwater did. There was a growing roar like that of an approaching train and a mass of seething muddy water came tearing upon us, bringing down rocks and boulders in its rush. Everybody raced for the bank and all but two made it. The last two men were bowled over and carried downstream. One was drowned, the other, with a broken leg and fractured ribs, managed to crawl ashore a mile lower down.

With the sound of the rain in my ears there was not a moment to lose. I had to get out of that stream-bed before the rain turned the earth into mud and made the banks unclimbable, and that could happen within minutes.

By the time I reached a lower stretch of bank it was already pouring and in the darkness I could scarcely see where I was driving. I put Zobeida straight at the bank and stepped hard on the accelerator. There were one or two moments of suspense when the wheels began to spin and I feared she would slip back, but she stuck to it gamely and we made it.

Now we were out in the open and in the thick of the storm. The lightning seemed to be sizzling all around me, while peal after peal of thunder crashed and crackled until my eardrums ached and the car vibrated from the noise of it.

I remained huddled on the seat, wondering what to do and doing nothing. I realised that Zobeida was the most prominent object in the whole landscape and, furthermore, was made of metal. To me it seemed that the storm was centred directly over the middle of the windshield. Following one blinding flash and simultaneous explosion, I could even smell the lightning, a heavy sulphurous odour, and I feared I might be blown to bits or carbonised any moment.

For an instant I gained consolation from the thought that of course the tyres, being rubber, would insulate me from the ground, but seconds later I remembered that the tyres were soaking wet, there could be no insulation, and my fears returned. For some minutes I pondered the advisability of getting out of the car, going some distance from it and lying flat on the ground, thereby making myself less conspicuous and letting Zobeida take the shock, if it came.

Between one line of thought and the other I spent a miserable time huddled in the car, keeping my hands off the wheel and my feet away from anything metal, with a stream of water running down my neck and a prayer on my lips that the storm would blow itself out and the turbulence move on somewhere else.

The noise and violence seemed to continue for hours, but actually the worst was over within half an hour. The crashing and crackling diminished and died away in a spiteful growling and rumbling, as it had begun, and as though the spirit of the tempest felt cheated of its prey and resolved to take it out on somebody else. The heavy clouds drifted away and surprisingly soon the sun was shining again. I relighted the stove, got the water boiling, and this time had an undisturbed meal.

The storm had passed, but its effects remained. From the nearby river-bed which I had vacated so hurriedly there now came a new sound, increasing in volume. I went back to look. From bank to bank the depression was a raging muddy torrent.

When Allah created the earth he had a lot of rock and rubble left over, so he flung it into a corner and that was Mekran. Thus say the Mekranis themselves and they ought to know, although the same story is told by their Beluch neighbours about their own country. From my personal experience of both, there is little to choose between them. Allah must have had a great deal of rock and rubble left over, for the whole of this region is just one tumbled mass of it.

For the most part the mountains run in an east-west direction, with one group forming the border of Afghanistan in the north, and other parallel ranges extending down to the Persian Gulf in the south. But every now and then erratic offshoots thrust jagged rocky spurs at tangents across the route.

The track was consistently bad and at frequent intervals I found the road blocked by landslides or boulders, which I had to clear away. In other places the trail had been washed away by floodwater, leaving deep channels which I had to fill in with rocks and stones.

Altogether I spent much time in road-building at this stage of the journey, but drew encouragement from the fact that I was on the last leg of the trip, and that barring unforeseen incidents I should reach Duzdab the next day.

An unforeseen incident was not long in occurring. I had been making reasonable progress in spite of the frequent stops for road repairs. At times the track had led across dried-up stream-beds, then down winding nullahs and over outlying rocky spurs. At one spot it entered a narrow ravine and here, for the first time since the Mil-i-Nadiri, I came upon traces of human handiwork.

Some old-time local ruler with an eye to the strategic possibilities of the position had fortified the crest and slopes of the spurs between which the track meandered, thereby effectively controlling the narrow defile. Fortunately the ancient masonry had eroded sufficiently to allow Zobeida to squeeze through, but the tricky passage itself was so narrow and winding that it seemed I would never be able to pass along it. I therefore left the car and made a long detour on foot to look for some other way round. But there was none. The old chieftain who chose this spot to bottle up the road knew what he was doing. The traffic could either pay the toll he demanded or it could turn about and go back to Iran or India, wherever it came from.

I too had no choice. I had to go on creeping through, with Zobeida tilted up on two wheels, first against one side of rock and then against the other, until we reached the last bend in the passage.

For one camel at least this must have been the straw that

broke his back, for there he lay, completely blocking the track at its narrowest point. He could not have been dead long, for the vultures had not yet discovered him, no doubt because he was concealed from view by the overhanging spur.

In the past I have had a good deal to do with camels and, with some notable exceptions, despite their superior air I have generally suspected them of harbouring a deep-seated grudge against the human race. This one must have nursed his spite until the very end, carefully selecting this particular spot to die where he could work the greatest mischief. No enemy saboteur could have done a more efficient job. Both location and timing were perfect. A few days earlier and the vultures would already have picked him clean, and the bleaching bones would have presented no obstacle.

Instead he lay complete, a mound of putrefaction distended to bursting point and stinking to high heaven, a sumptuous banquet for the carrion birds, who must have been busy elsewhere and had lost out to the swarms of bloated bluebottles, almost as loathsome as the horrid mess they battened upon.

Then followed one of the most revolting operations imaginable. With one hand holding a handkerchief to my nose and mouth, with the other I grasped the camel by one leg and tried to pull it round to a different angle. The carcase gurgled ominously and the bluebottles buzzed angrily round my head. I soon gave up the attempt, firstly because the carcase was too heavy for me to move with one hand and secondly, despite the handkerchief, the stench and the flies were overpowering.

Next I began collecting rocks, of which an abundance lay round about, and started to build a sloping ramp, forming a rough bridge over the bulge which was the carcase and down again on the other side. I had to discard the handkerchief while I did this and I tried holding my breath until my lungs were nearly bursting. Then I slowly edged Zobeida up the stone ramp. For a few horrible moments as the wheels passed over the bulging carcase and sank in, I thought it would explode and leave me stuck on top of it, and I actually began to vomit, but once again Zobeida played up and we made it safely. In another few yards we were out of the bottleneck, and in an open river-bed. Allah be praised! I could breathe freely again.

Next morning I was no longer breathing freely, thanks to a freshening breeze which filled the air and shrouded the sky with fine dust and grit. With visibility reduced to a bare one hundred yards and with no sun to guide me or clear track to follow, I could only grope my way in what I hoped was the right direction.

After some time the river-bed opened out and split into two branches. Immediately ahead the ground rose abruptly and the outline of a range of hills loomed out of the general greyness. It was a question of turning right or left.

I got out of the car and cast round on foot to try and pick up a track. There was little choice, but the way to the left seemed slightly more open and I followed it.

Now at last things began to go better. The wind dropped and while the air remained thick and dust-laden at ground level, the sky cleared and I could see the sun. More important, ahead and only a few miles distant I sighted an outstanding eminence. There was something vaguely familiar about it and from my map I knew it could not be anything other than Kuh Malik Siah.

The Peak of the Black Chieftain is a striking and useful signpost for travellers in this benighted region. As a mountain there is nothing remarkable about it. Its height of something less than four thousand feet makes it a mere pimple compared with the fourteen-thousand-feet Kuh-i-Taftan, a short crow's flight away to the south. But the fact that it rises abruptly from the plain gives it, like Gibraltar, an air of importance, almost grandeur, and makes it an outstanding landmark.

So the boundary-makers evidently decided when they fixed upon the Peak as the common meeting point of the Iranian and Indian empires with Afghanistan. For this reason, on a map the mountain stands out as prominently as it does in nature. At Kuh Malik Siah there was just one small hut with a flagpole and at the top of the pole a tattered and faded remnant which had once been a Union Jack. The hut was an Indian Government post, placed there to check on merchandise entering India by this remote back-door route.

The Indian clerk in charge seemed speechless with astonishment at my sudden appearance with Zobeida. He scrambled from the rough *charpoi* on which he had been lying half-naked, and hastily adjusted his dress. He was a friendly person, and over a glass of tea he bewailed his lot as a forgotten minion of the Raj, doomed to a term of solitude in this far-flung corner of the Empire.

He told me that such traffic as existed went by rail via Duzdab; only thieves and outlaws used the road and it was in very bad condition. I decided to take his advice and make for Duzdab. It was only a few miles to the south and I could not miss it. I had no fear of going astray for I had been there before. I gave the Indian a supply of cigarettes and we parted with a friendly handshake.

The going was still rough, but the air had cleared and the track was now well defined. Soon the hills receded around a flat expanse of hard, open plain. Across it in the distance I could see a collection of formless blobs dancing in the quivering air. In another quarter of an hour the mirage cleared, the blobs came down to earth, and I recognised the clustered buildings of Duzdab.

It was just about the most remote inhabited point in the Shah's dominions and the very name Duzdab reflected its loneliness. Translated it means Thieves' Water, so called because of a perennial spring of fresh water in the vicinity which in former times had been a frequent resort of roving bands of robbers and outlaws. (The name was later changed to Zahedan.)

The population of Duzdab was a very small one. There was an Iranian customs post to control merchandise and occasional travellers entering the country, and there was also an Iranian medical officer. The Indo-European Telegraph Company employed a permanent staff of signallers and maintenance engineers, and there was a European superintendent responsible for the running of the railway. At the time of my visit this officer was away somewhere up the line, and an Anglo-Indian station master was acting for him.

When I halted Zobeida outside the latter's office, he assumed at first that I had driven down from Sistan, or possibly even from Khorasan, but when I told him that I had not come from Meshed, but from Beirut via Baghdad and Kirman he stared at me with frank incredulity.

'D'you mean to say you drove all the way from Bayroot . . . in *that*?' The station master peered at Zobeida with a critical unbelieving eye.

I assured him that I had.

'Where *is* Bayroot?'

'On the Mediterranean.'

'My God,' he exclaimed with a strong Welsh accent. 'But man, how on earth did you get across the water?'

What more truthful and convincing answer could I have given than by a Ford! However, the man was genuinely interested and friendly, so I told him briefly of the route I had followed and asked him about the road ahead to Quetta. To my disappointment he shook his head. The road, he said, was quite unusable. Even at its best it had never been good, but after the recent rains whole stretches had been washed away, while in other places creeping sandhills had completely blocked it.

Chapter 19

DUZDAB (ZAHEDAN)

The station master urged me emphatically not to attempt the road. He pointed out that, although in case of trouble the train could pick me up, there would be no possible way of rescuing the car. The only solution, he assured me, was for both Zobeida and myself to entrain in Duzdab, where there was a proper car-loading ramp, and travel through as far as Spezand Junction, from where there was a good military road into Quetta.

The station master was obviously speaking from definite knowledge, and I had no alternative but to accept his advice. After all, I told myself, I was not making this trip as a stunt or to court publicity, still less was I attempting any record-breaking. I was told by others in Duzdab that in any case I held the record for being the first motorist ever to cover the last stage of this road from Kirman alone. Moreover, I now had to consider Zobeida more than myself. While I was confident that she herself could survive a further five hundred miles of severe ill-treatment, it was the tyres that worried me. I had no spares left, and the four in use were so cut and scarred they might collapse at any moment.

Now that I had crossed the territory of Iran and had reached its eastern limits, I felt that honour was satisfied. Besides, this was not my first experience of Beluchistan and I saw no particular merit in spending valuable time picking my way laboriously through it all once again. My own desire now was to reach Quetta with as little delay as possible.

From Duzdab I sent telegrams to the Consuls in Shiraz and Kirman, informing them of my safe arrival and thanking them once again for their hospitality and assistance. This would at least ease their minds and save them from sending out a search party.

Next day there was a train leaving for Spezand, and from the permanently constructed ramp I had no trouble whatever in embarking Zobeida. From the grimy, dust-covered seat of my compartment I watched the dismal landscape crawl by and realised the hopelessness of attempting to drive a car through it. I could see no signs of anything resembling a proper road. Nothing had changed in the years since I had last passed that way. Even the sun-bleached skeletons of animals, mainly camels, seemed just as numerous. The country appeared exactly as Allah had left it, and apart from the actual railway line Man had shown little desire to change it.

From Spezand it was only sixteen miles by road to Quetta and it would be quicker to drive than remain in the slowly moving train.

To feel Zobeida's wheels running smoothly along a proper surfaced road was like a dream, and I felt a great temptation to step hard on the accelerator and let her have her head, but this would have been tempting Providence too far. In one of the tyres the inner tube was beginning to bulge through the outer cover and, although only sixteen miles of good road now remained to our destination, the road surface was burning hot and the odds seemed heavily against our reaching Quetta without a blow-out. Could Zobeida possibly do it?

I drove slowly and had covered about half the distance when I sensed a certain bumpiness. I halted and inspected the tyres. Their condition was even more critical than I had thought, for that protruding inner tube was now bulging ominously and might explode any moment. Abdul would have sworn a *djinn* had got inside and would have exorcized it with *bismillahs*. I let some of the air out and hoping for the best started off again, driving even more slowly than before.

The remaining miles crept slowly by, five—four—three—two—one. We were now well within cantonment limits, and approaching the Quetta rest house. We reached the entrance and at that very instant there was a loud report. It set the bazaar dogs barking, sent a flock of green parrots screeching from the branches of a giant peepul tree, and brought the rest-house watchman out at a run.

The tyre had blown at last, but as we limped slowly to a halt, to me it could well have been a time-gun signalling the finish of a long-distance race. I felt jubilant with relief, for despite all the handicaps Zobeida had finally and safely completed the course.

POSTSCRIPT

Since it seemed I should be staying some time in India, I had arranged for certain extra baggage to be shipped by sea direct to Bombay. When I myself reached that city by train, the baggage had just arrived and I was able to clear it at customs.

Meanwhile, I had of course entered the country by the back door via Kuh Malik Siah and Beluchistan. As I have mentioned, there was a primitive government customs post at Kuh Malik Siah, but the Indian clerk-in-charge apparently had no instructions regarding anything other than local merchandise and he had passed my car and baggage through without query or inspection. Since I had my shotgun with me and the Indian authorities were particularly sensitive where firearms were concerned, I thought it proper to report this to the customs in Bombay.

The Indian customs official whom I approached was not quite sure how to deal with this unprecedented situation. He had never before encountered anybody arriving in India from Europe otherwise than by sea or, more recently, by air, and the following conversation ensued.

Customs Official: You say you brought the gun to India with you?

R.S.: Yes, that is so.

C.O.: But you did not come by P & O steamer?

R.S.: No.

C.O.: Then by what ship you came, please?

R.S.: I didn't come by any ship at all.

C.O.: Then you came by air.

R.S.: No, I didn't come by air.

C.O.: Then I am not understanding. If you did not come by sea, then you must have come by air. Isn't it?

R.S.: No, it isn't. I came overland.

C.O.: But you must have brought your car by ship, otherwise how could you get across the sea?

R.S.: I tell you I did *not* bring the car by ship. I drove it all the way. Ever hear of Kuh Malik Siah?

C.O. (*mystified*): No, Sahib.

R.S.: Well then, that's the way I brought it.

C.O. (*completely bewildered*): If you say so, it is no doubt correct, Sahib. And the gun is your own?

R.S.: It is my own.

C.O.: Then it can count as accompanied baggage, and there will be no duty.

R.S.: Thank you.

C.O.: But you must report it to the Bombay Police.

R.S.: Thank you, I will.

Two months later, I received an official communication from the Chief Inspector of Customs in Bombay. It read as follows:

> Reference: D.B. 12-bore shot-gun No 3964
> Please give number, make, and official markings of the aircraft by which you imported the above gun into India.

I replied briefly:

> Your letter of . . . date. Requested details as follows:
> FORD—A-MODEL—four wheels—black—
> Registration (Beirut)4271.

And that was the last I heard of it. That a stranger could enter India otherwise than by sea or air, and worse still could creep in by the desert backyard, armed with a shotgun, was evidently beyond Departmental comprehension.

My eventual parting with Zobeida was a somewhat poignant occasion. Had it been practicable, I would have liked to despatch her back to her original creators, who might have awarded her a place in their own particular Valhalla, or Hall of Fame. Unlike her royal namesake, whose tomb beside the Tigris perpetuates the memory of her bygone splendour, and unlike even the ass of Abdul, the Teller of Tales, whose relics were enshrined at least temporarily for public veneration, for this twentieth-century Zobeida no such honour lay in store. She left me at last to become the chattel of a native dealer in Quetta, to enter, probably, a period of menial duty beneath her deserts. I could not but reflect sadly that for her there would be no honourable ease in her old age, no respite, only work, or more likely over-work, before decrepitude ended in demise. Alas! for superannuated cars there is no gracious retirement, no sympathetic mechanic to minister to the ailments and stiffened joints of senility.

But Zobeida, indubitably, was the heroine of the journey and she shall not pass on without my grateful tribute to a faithful friend and companion. She stood by me stalwartly through thick and thin, heat and cold, desert and mountain defile, thunder- and dust-storm, and with equal fidelity had shown her stamina in difficulties such as no self-respecting car should be called upon to endure. Small wonder if she stalled at times . . . so did I. Happily for me, it was she that rallied first from the shock. She was more than once called upon to do the well-nigh impossible, but always won through.

Farewell Zobeida! *Requiescat in pace motorum*!